About The Author

Darren Smithson is owner and Managing Consultant of The Inform Group, a company he originally set up to provide business and development training, project management and educational services but is now becoming the vehicle for creating a new business and educational vision.

He has over 25 years working for or with the likes of IBM, BULL, NEC, The British Broadcasting Corporation and Microsoft, as well as with local government and community development organisations, but he is *not* like other business consultants.

He has delivered talks, training and workshops to audiences all over the world and to such organisations as the MOD, SITA, BA, the RAC, York Science College, Exeter University, The London Stock Exchange, Fujitsu-Siemens, CHS Ltd, Carpetright, Barnsley College and to a conference of 300 senior managers from Europe's largest IT companies ranging from IBM & Microsoft to Toshiba and Bull.

His talks are fast paced, fun, interactive and provocative and cover such esoteric topics as the multiple universe theory; what is life; what is intelligence and can we create it artificially; should robots have rights; is time travel possible; do aliens exist; where will we be in 50 years' time; how will technology affect our businesses, communities and schools; and are we humans merely parasites inhabiting a living organism? He has been described as being "like Prof Brian Cox- on steroids!"

On the more down to Earth side, he has sessions on time and prioritisation management, how to motivate you and your teams, goal setting and business planning, crime and safety basics, the need for alternate business practices, education and learning processes, why regeneration programmes fail, and the use of science to raise aspirations.

This book, and subsequent series, is the opening salvo in his new drive to change the way we live and work.

e: darren@theinformgroup.co.uk

 Darren Smithson   The Inform Group   @darreninform

Reviews of What Managers Don't Know

"A must have for all of us out there trying to wade through mud. Easy to read with lots of humour I found this a great read and really helpful. I also used it in my study! Makes a welcome change from the stuffy opinionated waffle that is out there."

"'What Managers Don't Know...' is an absolute revelation! The author engages the reader from the off with a no-nonsense, real-world approach to management and leadership. It's definitely top of my list for accessibility and relevance!

The workbook style allows the reader to really understand and apply the theories and concepts that Smithson writes about and this is a real stand out feature and certainly sets it apart from other books in its field."

"This book is full of really useful information, it's clear, concise and very easy to follow. The advice is backed up throughout and the author writes in a way that injects some humour into the text so it's a pleasure to read. I would recommend this book to anyone who would like advice on management and leadership issues. There are some great vouchers at the end of the book and I am looking forward to reading the next book in the series."

Copyright and Publishing Notices.

Copyright © TIGPress, 2015

The right of Darren Smithson to be identified as the author of this book has been asserted in accordance with the Copyright, Designs & Patents Act 1988. First published in 2012 by TIGPress and revised in 2015.
www.darreninform.com   email: info@theinformgroup.co.uk

All rights reserved. Except for the quotation of small passages for the purposes of criticism and review, no part of this publication may be reproduced, shared, stored in a retrieval system or transmitted in any form or by any means, electronic, mechanical, photocopying, recording, scanning or otherwise, except under the terms of the Copyright, Designs and Patents Act 1988 without the permission in writing of the author. Requests to the author should be emailed to darren@theinformgroup.co.uk. Brand and product names are trademarks or registered trademarks of their respective authors.

Preface to The Revised Edition

First off, let me put the record straight. I am not the CEO of some huge multi-national company. I'm not even a Managing Director of a huge multi-national company[1]. Hell, I never wanted to be. So what gives me the right to sit here and tell you what you don't know?

Simple. Working with CEOs and MDs from huge multi-national companies. Working with senior and middle management. Working with consultants. Working with staff, sales, support, engineers, programmers, community activists. Customers. Members of the public. Police. National and local government people and agencies. And through all of these experiences, I've seen the great, the good and the downright diabolical.

And, so as not to be all holier-than-thou, as a manager myself I'm guilty of some real humdinger mistakes- many of the ones in this book in fact! But I live by a simple philosophy: I never fail so long as I learn something new. It is one of my guiding principles, and one, which I hope you will see, that is embedded within the business principles included within this book.

This book is, therefore, my attempt to present to you what I've learned during my twenty-five years with some of the biggest or best (and not forgetting the worst) organisations in the UK and the world; to share some of those guiding philosophies that have developed during that time; and to present some strategies to enable you to become a better manager and leader, and for your organisation to become the best. Best for you, your customers, your shareholders and/or investors. But also best for your employees.

And isn't a world where everyone wins worth a look?

---

[1] But I have been through the pain barrier and have the scars to prove it.

30 Ideas

Taking the Diet ....

Introduction ....

Part One: Focus Areas

1. **Suspend your disbelief!** ....

    Enjoy the latest blockbuster? Did you believe a man could fly- or at the very least dodge bullets from 60 machine gun wielding lunatics? Then you're halfway to understanding the power of belief. You must *unlearn* Luke.

2. **Become your own expert!** ....

    They've got the certificates on the wall (or website) and the letters after their name, so they must know what they're talking about, right? Not in my experience they don't. So, never, ever, never, ever assume that the experts are right. Including me!

3. **Create a Vision!** ....

    Visions don't just belong to religious zealots and bored board rooms across corporate world, oh no, they are a fundamental necessity for your growth! *Honest!*

4. **Have a Plan!** ....

    Being ultra-positive and having a vision that will change the world is all well and good but without a plan of how to get there you won't believe how quickly you'll become lost.

5. **Play Nice!**

   Be a nice manager! Management isn't about telling people what to do; it's about enabling people to do it. You're there to support your team, not take the credit for their work.

6. **Walk the Talk!**

   Lead from the front, well, at least by example. You wouldn't catch Microsoft using Linux in-house so you'd better not be using some other time management system if you're selling your company's own time management system- or acting one way in business whilst promoting another.

7. **Everyone Works In Sales!**

   You can have the best sales team in the world but if everyone else in your organisation doesn't promote you, you will never maximise your potential!

8. **Waste Not, Want Not!**

   The best way to avoid cuts is to avoid waste in the first place. Review, mitigate, take note, avoid. Simples.

9. **Be a Marketing Magician!**

   The internet gives you free marketing! Well, yes, but only when you use it in conjunction with so-called traditional methods. The trick is to get the mix right- and then watch the magic take over.

10. **Run a Social Club!**

    People shouldn't view the place where they work as something that they have to do to pay the bills. You have to turn your workplace into somewhere where your employees feel they belong. A club so to speak.

11. **Up The Workers!** ....

All our ills aren't just down to bad management. Sometimes employees don't cover themselves in glory- resisting change for the sake of resisting is the surest way to lose your job, and not because you mark your card, but because the whole company goes bust. We have to learn a better way.

12. **Labelling the Point!** ....

When there's something to be said, say it everywhere. Make sure everyone in your organisation is not only aware of the message but completely understands it too.

13. **Become a Partner, Not A Product!** ....

Or choose a partner. Too often we work for the short term gain and fail to understand that a successful client is great for our business too, or finding a fantastic supplier can grow our business to new levels. So stop talking about customers and suppliers and talk about partners instead!

14. **Right Person for the Right Job!** ....

Would you task Jack the Ripper with running your Refuge for Homeless Women? Or put Genghis Khan in charge of international contracts? Yet many of us pull great salespeople off the floor and "promote" them to manager status even when the sales people tell us they don't want to be managers. Think about where you put your people.

15. **Work and Life in Harmony!** ....

Okay, so you've got this great smartphone platform so you can send your staff messages at midnight. Great isn't it!?! Well no. Studies show the more we encroach upon the social life of our employees the less productive they become. That means you too!

16. **The Customer's New Clothes!** ....

   The customer is King, but even kings need to be told when they're heading for the guillotine!

17. **Stimulation Through Diversity!** ....

   From cradle to the grave we're brought up in a world of conformity. We dress the same. We're taught the same. And we all fail the same. We must learn to be a team of individuals! Welcome to the Star Trek zone...

18. **Flex That Decision Making Muscle!** ....

   It's a world of punishment and humiliation when we get things wrong, so better not make a decision, right? Let someone else tell you what to do that way it's their fault when it all goes wrong. NO NO NO! Make decisions your friend, because being in control is better than having no control at all.

Part Two: The 12 Principles of Success

1. **The Caduceus Principle** ....

   Medics talk about prevention is better than the cure! It's time we all became doctors!

2. **The Maverick Principle** ....

   We have to jump on that loud mouth who keeps finding things wrong with the way we run our business don't we? Not if you want to survive long term you don't. Embrace your inner rebels.

3. **The Jewish Vampire Principle** ....

   Question: would a crucifix work on a Jewish vampire? Despite what Buffy lore tells us we must be careful and use the right tools for the right job. And that includes the right people tool. I mean too.

4. **The Court Jester Principle** ....

Let's ban laughter in the workplace! I mean, how can people be productive if they're too busy having fun. *Honestly.* I'm being sarcastic by the way.

5. **The Round Table Principle** ....

Have you put in place the facilities for everyone in your organisation to share their ideas, news, gossip, experiences? No? Then you're really missing out.

6. **The Unexpected Guest Principle** ....

What event, however unlikely, should it happen send your company into non-existence? If you don't ask this question on a regular basis you could find yourself in big trouble. Just ask those who worked in the vinyl industry. *What* industry!?!

7. **The Chameleon Principle** ....

Evolution not revolution! Adapt or die! Yet we still often cling to the belief that what got us this far will enable continued success. No, we must continually grow and change to succeed: or we could put our heads in the sand and become lunch. Or a dodo.

8. **The Prometheus Principle** ....

I am the god of hellfire, and I bring you fire!! A bit OTT? Maybe. But if you don't create the spark someone else will. And he/she who controls the fire, wins. Just ask onDigital.

9. **The Einstein Principle** ....

What's a scientist doing in a book about business? Einstein was a great thinker and philosopher and a lot of his musings are directly applicable to the business community. Besides, you can impress your friends at parties.

10. **The Confucius Principle** ....

Learning, education, training and development. All must be fostered, supported and engaged in. Or you could just hire unthinking robots. Your choice.

11. **The Gaia Principle** ....

Your business or organisation is a living, breathing entity. If you don't view it in a holistic and nurturing way then you can seriously stunt its growth. Feeding isn't enough. You have to support it, encourage it and keep it whole.

12. **The 99 Monkeys Principle** ....

What's better? To be a trend setter or a follower of trends? By understanding this simple principle you can dramatically improve your organisations viability. And yes, there really were 99 monkeys. Plus 1.

Conclusion

Next steps ....

Final Words ....

Taking the Diet

Every chapter of this book contains food for thought. Simply read one chapter a day and act on the exercises or ideas contained therein and fill your mind with positive or stimulating concepts and lessons to help you change your focus, improve your mind, enhance your learning- or even change your life.

Each chapter is also laid out like a five course meal of information and features.

- *The Main Text*. The actual chapter itself, discussing, teasing or harassing you with ideas and true stories of real events.
- *Try something else*. If an idea looks like being more than an appetiser then add to the flavour by reading a related chapter. *Try something else* guides you to a related tip to expand and enhance the flavours of the first. Yes, I am a foodie. Whatever gave you that idea?
- *Take a bite*. Give it a taste – simple activities to get the cauldron boiling.
- *Words of Wisdom*. Why just listen to one chef, here you'll find words by other luminaries who have something important to say.
- *Coping with Indigestion?* If at first you bake the cake and it rises fantastically well, please try to hide your amazement. If, on the other hand, you still think its going to come out like a rock cake you'll find a Q & A that highlights common problems and suggests a recipe for improvement.

For all the managers, good, bad and ugly, who gave me so much material to call upon. You know who you are!

And for my beautiful daughters, Frances & Rachael, who I hope will learn from my mistakes and the mistakes of others.

And for Miss Bonnie, for adding gasoline to the fire.

Introduction

"The problem with being in the rat race is that even if you win, you're still a rat."
Lily Tomlin

I hate my job. My workers are always taking the piss. My manager just doesn't know what he's doing!

A New Beginning!

In July 2012, I released my first version of this book, under the title "What Managers Don't Know & Workers Can't Tell Them". I knew nothing about publishing books, and simply wrote and published the book in the hope that people would read it and begin to help me change the world. Since then however, I have learned a great deal about publishing books and so decided now was the time to rethink both the positioning of the book, and its importance to my business model.

One of driving factors behind this were positive comments made by people who did buy the book, many of them saying they hadn't realised that the book was not just about management techniques, but also helped them become better leaders, or even gave them a roadmap for creating their own business.

So, I have renamed this book to reflect that depth of subject more, and also created a series of extra "What Managers Don't Know" e-books (around 80-100 pages typically), which saw publication from March 2014. I also used it as an opportunity to update some of the text and correct some formatting issues. If you bought the first version of this book, you do not need to buy this one. However, if you're new to the WMDK brand, you're in at the start of something I hope will become very special and I commend you for taking your hard earned pennies and spending them with me.

Three Typical Groups

If you're reading this book you probably belong to one of three groups of people.

You could be a manager, either of senior or middle position, or an entrepreneur setting up a new business, who is at least forward-thinking enough to take a look at new ideas, or curious enough to make sure that you're not missing anything that could give your competitors (whether business competitors or internal threats to your own position) an advantage. You want to make sure you take advantage of any new thinking and you may also heard of several trends that are taking root in the business world, and you are trying to find out if they are something you or your company should take a serious look at, or if there are other more important considerations to take into account.

Or, you may be a worker who every now and again puts your head over the parapet and thinks; *I could do a better job of running this company than these morons*. You have firm ideas and opinions but feel that they are not being listened to. Furthermore, you are probably aware of a vague feeling that your life isn't quite right, that maybe you give so much of yourself to working-life that you don't have enough energy left for your personal life. Maybe you've decided to check it out to see if there's something you can use to help you define these vague feelings of wrongness, or if there are any ideas in this book that can change, for the better, the way your organisation works with its employees.

Or you could belong to the group of managers; either senior or middle, or union officials, or employees who have turned up for work this morning and found a copy of the book surreptitiously placed on your chair, or on your desk in front of your computer screen. You have no idea what it's about, who left it and why. If you find yourself in this group then I have bad news for you: you're in trouble.

Because this book is about how companies and individuals in management fail to understand what truly motivates people; how they can take the best that their people offer but then utilise it in completely the wrong way; how in the race to beat the competition they neglect their greatest asset; and how, by doing these things, they eventually cause their (or should that be *your*?) business great harm.

And for those in the workforce feeling very smug at the moment, it's also about how your lack of active and positive participation in your company's future means you will have to keep your own resume up-to-date, just in case!

By the end of this book, I hope that both management and workers will understand why you have to work better together, what resources and processes are already there to help you do just that, and what 12 guiding principles you MUST adopt to thrive in the business world of the 21st century.

But before we go into that, let's first introduce the key problem facing businesses today.

The Problem

At this point I feel like Douglas Adams trying to describe "space" in The Hitchhikers Guide To The Galaxy:

"Space is big. Really big. You just won't believe how vastly, hugely, mindbogglingly big it is. I mean, you may think it's a long way down the road to the chemist's, but that's just peanuts to space."

Now, superimpose the words "the problem" for space and you'll start to get a feel for what is wrong with the way that business conducts itself today. The problem with trying to define the problem is that it is so complex that really, it isn't a single problem at all, but rather a series of interlaced misconceptions, incorrect assumptions and bad practices. So whilst "working as a team" is one important aspect to an organisation's continued success, it cannot be seen in isolation, just as you wouldn't look at only cost-cutting exercises to maintain profitability in a tough economic climate… oh, I just realised, that's exactly what many companies do *do*!

No! What we must learn to do is chunk the problems and opportunities and challenges down into different categories and sub-groups or projects. But don't just address one solution or proposal. Educate yourself to understand that problems are here to stay and diversify and that no-one solution will work on them all and you are at least ready to read on.

Why Me?

As I write this, I can hear many of you asking what gives me the right to criticise/debate/challenge/suggest the issues that we're all interested in here. First of all, let me say that if you don't like what you read within because it makes for uncomfortable reading, don't come complaining to me. You see, this book isn't my fault. It's yours.

If I had my way, this would be a fantasy novel called "Wizards", a book I've been writing for some time now. But over the last decade I've experienced growing unease about the way that the business community, in its widest possible term, runs itself. More and more this unease has grown into definable issues and questions… questions that I've been forced to try and answer myself as I found that management either couldn't, or wouldn't, answer them, and that the workforce were either unable, or afraid, to articulate. So you see this book is a case of "if you want a job doing… do it yourself."

In fact, when I started writing this book we were not aware of the full extent of just how bad our business and political leaders were. We didn't know about the LIBOR fixing, the £13 trillion hidden by the richest people to escape tax, the callous disregard with which politicians treat individuals as statistics to keep the markets happy (so that *some* individuals can stay rich) and just how much the world's current economic crisis is being manipulated by a few powerful individuals and organisations so they can make obscene profits out of our misery. If I thought things needed to change before we learned all this, imagine how I feel now.

Not that I'm saying I'm a perfect manager or entrepreneur. Trust me, if there's a mistake to be made, I've made it. But I learn from *everything* and this book is a distillation of those experiences into a set of ideas and guiding principles. And I had to do this book because by and large, the vast majority of our business leaders and managers fundamentally *don't understand what motivates people*, or how to make the most of the assets they have.

Indeed, originally I was going to title the book "You're having a laugh aren't you?" Oooohh I can just imagine that there are now some folded arms out there. Don't worry. I just wanted a title that made sure I had your attention, seeing as you read this it's probably still relatively early in the morning (you may be on the tube or train, or even have found this book waiting for you as I said previously) or late at night (you're sat up in bed hoping that this business book someone suggested might send you to sleep. It won't, although it might give you nightmares.)

One final thing. You've probably already notice that this book is not written in the style of a normal business book. That's because it isn't a normal business book. I'm not a normal business consultant. I'm a Rebel in The FDG.[2] So let's kick back, pour a drink (or make a cuppa depending on the time of day) and get started.

---

[2] F^*&ng decadent generation, WASP.

Part One. Focus Areas

If we regard the 12 Principles as a banquet, these 18 areas of focus are the recipes you need to follow to make the feast a success.

We recommend that you try out a couple at a time to get them embedded in your psyche so that you don't over-stuff yourself.

1

Suspend Your Disbelief!
Time to start believing in yourself

Full of self doubt? Here's why it's important to start every change from a sense of total belief. And if you can't find that total belief just yet, how you can fake it!

Have you ever been in a place where you were simply awesome? Where everything just clicked and you felt you could do absolutely anything? I bet you have. You might not remember straight away, but keep digging- somewhere, at some time, you rocked.

So why is it most of us believe we can never do anything right!? Why do we focus on when we screwed up, or embarrassed ourselves, or failed massively? It's because we humans are deletion creatures- our brains have to cope with so much input, both from our external senses and from within our own body system, that if we couldn't filter most of it out, we'd go insane.

But hand in hand with that goes another well-known axiom; that of the pleasure-pain principle. Now, we all think we understand what is meant by that oxymoron but do we really? In fact, we are ALL driven by two overriding needs; the need to avoid pain and to gain pleasure. Tony Robbins has a fantastic take on this[3], and his conclusion is staggeringly troublesome: we will do more to avoid pain than we will to gain pleasure.

So when we feel the need to take any kind of action- even something as changing our beliefs- our brain will evaluate how much pleasure we might get against how much pain we might have to take. It will almost always choose to avoid the pain if it thinks it could be significant, even though the rewards (i.e. the pleasure) might be huge!

This is why when you wanted to ask the girl/boy out on a date, even though you knew they were simply the best, you didn't- because you feared that you would be rejected and experience the pain of humiliation! It's why you didn't leave a relationship even though you knew it was a bad one, because deep down you associated more pain with leaving than staying (even if that association was one of fear of reprisal if you did leave). It's even why you didn't apply for the better job, which had more pay and more favourable conditions; you simply weren't experiencing enough pain in your current job to risk getting a 'thank you but no' letter in the post.

So we allow fear to convince us to rationalise that we're not that good anyway. And so we don't try.

Feel the force, Luke!

We must get rid of the belief, therefore, that we aren't good enough; indeed any similar beliefs- that is, those beliefs that limit us- must be unlearnt right away. NOW! Not tomorrow. Think you're a no-hoper, then you are. Think you're a bad person, then you are. Think you can't do it, then you're right, you can't. Whatever we think, we are. Or

---

[3] For full details you should check out his PowerTalk audio book "The Six Human Needs."

become. Or do. That's because our brain doesn't want to make you out to be a liar, so if you believe you're a jackass, then that's what you'll become.

Take a bite...

Right now, grab a piece of paper and write down a description of at least five times you felt totally self-confident, those times when you just blew away all problems or objections and totally achieved what you wanted; it might be that really awesome business presentation you did, or when you asked out that cute boy/girl who said yes, or even convincing little Johnny to tidy up his bedroom! Capture the details, how you felt, what you were doing; did you stand in a certain way or have a particular breathing pattern going on? Then once you've done that, fold it up and put it in your wallet or purse, to be brought out and reviewed whenever you're about to tackle something you feel anxious about. And add to it each new success! Pretty soon, you'll have all the evidence you need, there in black and white, to persuade your brain that you absolutely can do what it is you want to do!

If we're going to give our brain something to think about therefore, why not make it something big, something positive, tell yourself with utter conviction that you are going to move that *toe* (am I the only person that remembers this John Wayne[4] movie???), and you will. Why? Because, as I said, your brain doesn't want to make you out to be a liar!

If you're like me, you go to the movies to escape, to have fun and forget about the real world for a while. Art movies have their place, and Schindler's List may well be an emotional kick in the pants, but if I'm taking the trouble to go out I want to be entertained! For me this usually means Bruce Willis taking on a skyscraper full of terrorists in his

---

[4] Wings of Eagles (1957)- all together now: "I'm gonna move that toe! I'm gonna move that toe!"

bare feet or Jeff Goldblum uploading a computer virus onto the alien mothership.

But to be entertained in the face of such preposterous suppositions – why does the alien mothership run a Mac compatible computer as an example[5]- then I, and billions like me, have an inbuilt skill- we can suspend our disbelief (see, how everything *does* eventually knit together?).

Try something else...

For more on the power of words and labels on our beliefs, see Principle 7: The Chameleon Principle.

The trick is to take that cinema-trained skill and learn to use it in real world scenarios. Okay, so you haven't had training in how to stand in front of 300 people and excite them about your latest idea, but if this were a movie and you were Bruce Willis, you'd just wing it anyway and save the day! In other words, if you find yourself believing something negative about yourself, suspend it for a couple of hours and be entertained instead.

Cultivate your garden

If it's simply a matter of believing in yourself then why don't more people do it? It's because our beliefs are constantly being shaped and influenced by those around us. You must be careful what you allow your mind to cultivate; small seeds can become great big forests so make sure you grow healthy trees. Purge doubts from your mind as they

---

[5] Actually, the alien computer had rendered itself vulnerable by adapting its programming to send signals out to our communications satellites so it could orchestrate the invasion countdown. I worked this out all by myself.

appear (these act like weeds in a garden!) and instead replace them with great ideas, focus on good memories and positive experiences.

Then start to create that new belief in who you are. If you're a long way from what you want to be, then define that person in detail, write it down- this is who you must become, and then act as if you were that person already. You'll be amazed at how your focus will change, and how your confidence will improve. Walk like that person would walk, talk like them, stand (or sit) like that person would. If you're unsure what that would be, then look around for role-models who are like the person you would want to be, and see how they act.

Then take that positive new self-belief and whilst in this awesome state, make those changes that you know you need to make. Tell your boss you deserve a raise, or go kiss that person you're dreaming of, with so much passion that their toes curl (and then simply walk away with a wink before they have time to speak- can you imagine how much *their* state would be changed??).

Or, if you're not quite ready yet for something so major, start small, try out other ideas in this book- build on your successes to support your new self-belief (add them to your list!) and get ready to rock your world. And the world of those around you.

Words of Wisdom...

If you believe in magic, you will have a magical life.
ME!

Coping with indigestion?

Q: Well, okay, I understand that having a strong sense of self-belief is a good thing, and I'm a really positive person, but I still don't seem to be making any headway in my life. What am I doing wrong?

A: *Ah, that's because a strong belief system on its own isn't enough. Standing in your garden saying "I don't believe in weeds, I don't believe in weeds- there just aren't any weeds!" won't stop your garden from being overrun with weeds[6]! You have to support your beliefs with strategies and action. Conversely though, you can **use** your beliefs to support those actions and strategies. Choosing the right strategies is also vitally important! But we'll deal with that later in the book.*

Q: **You say that our beliefs are constantly influenced by those around us, I consider myself to be intelligent and would surely be able to filter any undue influence?**

A: *You'd be surprised about how simple it is for your brain to programme itself without you even realising- and it can have major impact on your life! For example, at school, I was constantly told by a teacher I was rubbish at maths. So I became rubbish at maths because I believed I was rubbish at maths! And I stayed rubbish at maths for decades because I believed what my teacher told me. I even made career choices based on this belief. And I too am considered to be fairly intelligent. D'oh!*

I'll explore the role of experts in the next chapter.

Q: **All this is well and good but what does it have to do with running a business?**

A: *Before you can change your organisation, you have to start with changing yourself! Furthermore, although this chapter looks at the micro (i.e. you) the principles and coping techniques can easily be transferred to the macro (i.e. the organisation), but it is best to start small and learn from mistakes (or create new distinctions) before jumping right in. After all you wouldn't do brain surgery after watching an episode of Casualty would you?*

---

[6] This is an adaptation of an example given by Anthony Robbins- I could come up with one of my own but really, this is such an effective example, why would I bother?

2

Become Your Own Expert!

A second opinion ain't enough!

Whenever we need to make an important decision our natural instinct is to call upon the advice of an expert. Every now and again we might even look for a second opinion. But we should never follow blindly the advice given by an expert. Or experts.

Who do you believe? Why do you believe them? When our Doctor says we should take the medicine, how many of us actually question it?

First you should ask yourself, what have the experts ever done for us? Oh sure, we've become the most advanced species in the known universe, and some of the medical and scientific breakthroughs have been awe-inspiring. We might even have bought a fantastic HDTV that makes going to the cinema a thing of the past. But there is a flip side to listening to experts. After all, it's experts who gave us thalidomide, the atom bomb, political correctness- not to mention a ruined world economy. You see the truth is, experts get it wrong. And if you follow their advice blindly, you could find yourself in a whole world of problems. Just ask all those who lost their jobs and homes in the 2008 Banking Crisis and the resulting era of austerity.

When my maths teacher (yes I mean *you* Mr D of Felkirk Middle School!) told me I was rubbish at mathematics and would never amount to much in any job that needed numeric skills, I believed him. After all, he was the Mathematics Teacher, *the expert*. I believed him so much I struggled for the rest of my school life in the subject, taking three attempts to get a mathematics O Level. Worse, I chose a career path based on the assumption that I was no good at mathematics.

However, something strange happened after I'd been working for a few years. It started with my ability to take any piece of technology, understand it and extrapolate out the potential long term benefits of that piece of technology. Even better, I found I could explain back what those benefits would be, and why, in terms that non-technical people could understand. I became an "acknowledged expert", hired out by my employers to clients to show them how our company could benefit them. Slowly I built up enough references to start to challenge the opinion fostered within me by my old teacher, because many of these pieces of technology involved bits and bytes and cycles per second. In other words, I was converting numbers into opinions.

Then I discovered I could do the same with scientific concepts, understanding the principles behind some pretty esoteric theories to do with temporal physics, quantum teleportation and general relativity. So I started a science degree with the Open University and found that, with some expertly written and presented "how to" mathematic sections within the course materials, actually I was pretty good at mathematics! Pretty soon I was calculating planetary orbits, tectonic plate movements and the potential power unlocked by $e=mc^2$.

I came to realise that it wasn't me who was rubbish at maths, it had been my maths teacher who had been rubbish at teaching *me*!! But by then, I was well down the line of a career path that made it almost impossible to turn back. Don't let your life become a slave to the opinion of an expert!

Take a bite...

I want you to write down five times in the past that you have had experts tell you what you should do. Then note if they were right or wrong.

Then write down five times when you did your own research before making a decision. As before, note if you were right or wrong.

Bet there's not much difference is there?

The truth is, becoming an expert means building up references (or experiences, or knowledge learned via schooling etc) that back up the opinion that one is an expert in a particular field. Being an expert therefore, if you strip away all the mechanics and processes, is all about *opinion*. There is no reason why you cannot form an educated opinion from conducting your own research.

Am I saying ignore advice from experts- absolutely not! Am I saying that you should at least gain some knowledge about a particular issue/problem/opportunity before you simply accept what you're being told? Yes, absolutely.

Anyone can make a mistake![7]

Opinions and beliefs can be wrong. Even if they are given in complete faith by an expert, they can still be wrong. You should check the facts, and depending on the importance of the decision you may face, get a second, third, fourth opinion, and then, and only then, form an opinion of your own.

For example, Warren Buffett is one of the world's richest men, and he made his fortune by playing the stock markets since the 40's. He is widely regarded as one of the most successful investors of all time and

---

[7] Said the Dalek as he climbed off the dustbin.

his advice has been sought by Presidents of countries and companies both. Yet, as Buffett is willing to admit, even the best investors make mistakes.

In 2008, Buffett bought a large stake in the stock of Conoco Phillips as a play on future energy prices. Given the state of the energy market at that time, one would think that an increase in oil prices was likely over the long term and therefore Conoco Phillips would benefit. However, this turned out to be a bad investment, because Buffett bought in at too high of a price, resulting in a multibillion-dollar loss to his investment firm, Berkshire. The difference between a great company and a great investment is the price at which you buy stock, and this time around Buffett was, as he put it, "dead wrong." Since crude oil prices were well over $100 a barrel at the time, oil company stocks were already way up.

In effect, in this instance, even Warren Buffett succumbed to the excitement of a big rally and bought in at a price that was already too high. In other words, he let his emotions rule his intellect, and lost lots of money. And because he was the expert at stock market game play, many other investors did the same! Some investors however did not, because they analysed the situation for themselves, coming to the conclusion that the price of crude oil has always exhibited tremendous volatility and that oil companies have long been subject to boom and bust cycles.

A couple of years ago I finally got enough of a lump sum of money together to make some investments. Most people in my shoes would normally find a local or recommended stock broker to invest that money. I actually spent time first doing some research and was astounded to realise that a stock broker gets his commission on a deal regardless of whether you lose money on it or not! And he/she gets more commission when you sell the stock to try and stem your losses![8]

---

[8] Actually, you don't really lose or gain money until you sell so it's all relative.

I didn't like that idea much so decided to at least get a passing knowledge of how to choose stocks. Along the way I found out about a great money making exercise called "channelling" – I won't go into what this is because this book isn't about making money on the stocks – so my plan was this: build up enough money through a buy and hold strategy, and when the markets stabilise, take some of that money and use it to generate short-term income by employing the channelling strategy. I therefore needed a stock broker who could provide me with the tools at a later date to move my money around and control my channelling stocks.

It took me weeks of calls to find a stockbroker (and this included many high street banks offering stock market policies) to find one who knew what channelling was! The good news is that my buy and hold shares beat the markets; but I took those investments and decided to invest in setting up my business instead. Once I am certain I have stability of income, I'll start the process again. Don't get me wrong, I don't consider myself an expert on the stock market, but I am informed about the choices and tools available.

And you must do the same when it comes to launching or managing a business.

Expert Advice for Work

All the preceding is equally true about how you approach things for your work life. It doesn't matter if you're just setting up in business, working within a large organisation, or own said organisation. Experts (often called consultants) are everywhere! And all of them say they are right, even when they differ from each other. So who do you believe?

Words of Wisdom...

For every expert there is an equal and opposite expert.
Attributed to Arthur C. Clarke.

You have to learn to believe in yourself. I know that sounds trite but the fact remains: experts can only offer their opinion. True, it may be an opinion based on experience, but opinion can be wrong. So start with your idea or approach, read books, ask questions, hire consultants to do the research and propose/train/deliver the strategies and changes.

Try something else...

Getting many opinions and doing your own research is all well and good, but eventually you have to make a decision. See Idea 18: Flex That Decision Making Muscle!

But don't just take their word for it. Check it out. Look at differing opinions. Check your gut. Yes, that's right; I'm firmly saying bring emotion and intuition into business. If something just doesn't feel right, there's a good chance that it isn't.

By the way, I am fully aware of the irony of this chapter; after all, aren't I saying I'm an expert and asking you to listen to my advice? Well, sort of. I'm also clear however that I don't have all the answers, I'm still formulating new distinctions and ideas and strategies and tools, and whilst everything in this book works for me, it might not all work for you. All I'm asking therefore, is that you try the ideas in this book and perfect the ones that work for you.

The Paralysis of Analysis

However, a word of warning! Once you start fishing around and getting various opinions from different experts, you could find yourself trapped in a mire of conflicting data. One need only look at the constant claim and counter claim about dieting and nutritional needs! What's worse, the more you research the more you seem to build up arguments on many sides- and we humans can often decide not to make a decision because what if it's the wrong one? After all, the experts can't even agree!

This is called the "paralysis of analysis" and must be avoided at all costs. After all, as it says in the Rush song "Freewill"- "If you choose not to decide you'll still have made a choice!"[9]

No, before you start the odyssey of opinion assessment, set yourself an end date for when you will make a final decision, and stick to it. We'll talk more about the power of decisions in Chapter 18, in the meantime remember this: *become your own expert*. It'll make you more careful about making rash decisions because no-one likes to be blamed, especially when you come to blame yourself!

Coping with indigestion?

Q: Okay, I get the message, but surely there are limits? After all, if I have to go for brain surgery I can't become an expert in brain surgery without years at med school, can I?

A: *No, but you can become versed in the illness that means you have to have brain surgery in the first place. Is brain surgery the only option? Is it the best option? What are the upsides and downsides of this verses any alternatives? Remember, people tend to diagnose based on their area of expertise- a surgeon will want to cut, a chemist will want to drug, a spiritualist will want to put their hands on your body... well, okay I made that last bit up, but you get the point.*

Q: But what if I ignore the expert and make the wrong decision?

A: *That's why it's important to get more than one opinion, so that you can weigh up the evidence and make an informed choice. Will you always be 100% right, no of course not, but are the experts always 100% right? We'll talk more about the power of decisions later.*

---

[9] From the rather excellent LP Permanent Waves, one of those albums everyone should have.

3

Create A Vision!
Know what you want!

People think that "visions" only belong to corporate boardrooms or religious zealots who've been in the desert too long, but to think so is to ignore a fundamental law of the universe: if one doesn't have one's own vision then one will be striving towards someone else's vision.

For the most part, many of us encounter visions whilst working for some corporation or government organisation. And for the most part, visions are boring, bear little relation to the reality of the wider organisation and become nothing more than a plaque behind the reception wall. But we shouldn't be so quick to dismiss how powerful a vision can be at creating real excitement and momentum and become a driver for change!

Stop and consider- when you've been at your best, at your most unstoppable, hasn't that been when you've had a clear idea of what it was you wanted or needed to achieve? You weren't willing to quit until the job was done, or take no for an answer, or be slowed down by the negatives coming from others. And these successes have arisen from ad hoc and very narrow visions of what you were aiming for- just think therefore about how much more effective you would be if you had a clear vision for *all* of your life!

The same is true for your business.

It doesn't matter what kind of business it is- corporate, SME, 3rd sector, statutory agency, new or start up, one person band, you must have a vision for what it is you want to do. And your vision must excite you, and if you have employees it must excite *them* too.

Make Your Vision So That It Moves You!

I already mentioned in the last chapter that we should bring emotion into the business world. That goes against everything we are taught about business, particularly in the UK. But emotion is good when used in the right places.

And no-where more so than when deciding on the vision for your business.[10]

For example, how many of us have seen a Vision like this one:

> "XYZ Corporation will be the best widget maker in the country by 2020."

Would you feel excited about working for a company with this vision? Would you jump out of bed every morning thinking "Zowie! I just can't wait to get to work and make those widgets!"? I think not.

And yet, this is how consultants often direct organisations to think about what a vision should be: do what it says on the tin.

Or how about this kind of Vision:

---

[10] Or department, or team, or company, or organisation. From this point on wherever you see the words "your business", "your organisation" or "your company" etc I mean all of the above.

"ABC Corporation will strive to exceed all expectations for customer service and product excellence whilst meeting the financial obligations due its shareholders and achieving primary market dominance."

Great! Isn't it? It's not? Why not? Oh, it's just board-speak that bears no relationship to what you do on a day to day basis? You know what? You might just be right!

And yet, again, go to vision & goal setting (or business planning) workshops run by some of the biggest consultancy companies in the world and that is exactly how you will be told to construct a Vision.

So, if you are a board member, can you see how these kinds of visions just don't connect with anyone other than other board members?

If you're not a board member but work in a company with these kinds of visions, start suggesting improvements. Show them this chapter! Anything to stop businesses from perpetuating these do it today and then forget about it today visions.

Words of Wisdom...

Where there is no vision, people perish.
Proverbs 29:18

Your company vision therefore should follow these simple rules:

1. It MUST be in plain English.
2. It MUST use emotive language. I'm not suggesting you go down the route of "we will rip the faces off the competition", but choose words that excite, motivate and create momentum.
3. Take the Vision out of the board room. Get staff/clients/partners involved- in fact, let them take the lead.
4. Don't try to make it perfect from the off.

For example, for my company, I have been tinkering with TIG[11]'s Vision since I started. When I first wrote this book it stood at:

> "The Inform Group is here to enable you, our clients, to be the best you can be and everything we do comes from that simple premise. We are setting the standard for business and learning services and we want work and learning to be fun, ethical and beneficial for all. We define success and greatness in these terms."

Now, you'll notice before I typed out the Vision, I said "it stood at" and that I've been "tinkering" with the Vision. Yes, that's right, tinkering. The reason for this is that I'm still not happy that it is strong enough and your Vision should always be looked at and improved upon on a regular basis (check out the latest version at www.darreninform.com).

Take a bite...

If your current company vision doesn't make you feel like getting up on a morning, scrap it and start again. If you haven't got a vision, take a stab at one. Then ask people what they think. Refine it. If you have people working for you, email to them all and explain that you don't think it's right either. Run workshops and get your employees involved, including temporary staff and your cleaning staff. Above all keep the language simple but emotive. Make the whole process an event! And follow up on the outcomes on a regular basis.

There are many reasons for this. Firstly, it both reminds AND reinforces within yourself, your management team, your staff, partners and clients what your organisation is here to do.

---

[11] TIG is the affectionate name for The Inform Group.

Secondly, it allows you to tweak the Vision so that it becomes even more of a motivator, or even to capture any changes in your market or organisational focus.

Thirdly, it reminds everyone (and subconsciously installs the belief) that the organisation is a living, breathing and changing entity, and as such, change is part of the order of life and should not be feared.

For myself, I am still not happy with my company Vision. It's almost right; it says what we do, how we plan to do it and what our ethos as an organisation is. But it still isn't perfect. It probably never will be, but it is a good starting point (though may be different when you read now)!

Everyone Owns Your Vision

One of the main points about creating a Vision for your organisation is that it must be shared by everyone connected to your organisation. It must come out of the board room (or executive lounge, or reception plaque or entrepreneurial head) and be owned by the people who work for or with you.

But it shouldn't stop there. It should be shared with your suppliers and customers. Or, as I prefer to call them, your partners and, if you must, your clients[12].

You can even turn it into a PR opportunity by bringing your clients into the process. Have an event where you wine and dine your clients (or potential clients) and don't sell to them. Instead, show them your Vision, explain the ethos behind it and ask them for their feedback. Position your organisation as the one that wants to truly align with the needs of its clients. Don't try to sell them a thing at the event.

And when you, or your sales people or customer service staff, call them, they'll remember that your approach is so much different from that of

---

[12] I prefer to view my clients as partners also

competitors. In short, you will have achieved TOMA! (that's Top Of Mind Awareness).

Try something else...

Once you have got your vision, that's great. But a vision without a plan of how you're going to make it real is just a dream. See the next chapter for what you should do next!

More Words of Wisdom...

"If you can dream it, you can do it. Remember this whole thing was started by a mouse."
Walt Disney

Coping with indigestion?

Q: I've always been told that a vision should say what it does on the tin, but you're saying that I should show emotion in it instead?

A: *Not exactly. Your vision should definitely relate to what it is that your organisation does and, importantly, refer to where you want to be ultimately. But the language should definitely stir emotions- if you can create passion in yourself and your employees with it, you are more likely to succeed.*

Q: Aren't visions just something you do for your company report?

A: *No. It IS true that too many organisations "do" a vision simply because they feel they should have one from a vague marketing and PR sense, but they miss the point. The vision is the reason why you, and your employees, are doing it in the first place!*

4

Have a Plan!

Know where you want to go and how to get there!

Having a Vision for your business, a great service or product to sell/deliver, and wonderful people to work with is all well and good if you don't actually know what to direction to go in and what actions you need to take.

After all, if you decide to go on a sponsored charity walk around the world you wouldn't just set off without first considering which direction to set off in, what paper work you'll need, where you'll need to do more than walk (oceans don't make the best place to walk over) and so on. At the very least, find out where the minefields are!

At this point I would normally refer to a study conducted by Yale in 1953 where researchers spent a day with a class to found out how many of them had written goals for their life. It was, it was reported, about 3%. In 1973, they supposedly contacted the class members and did a follow up survey. Of the survivors, the 3% were financially better off than the other 97% combined.

Unfortunately it now looks like the study, referred to for decades by speakers and writers the world over, never actually occurred.[13] Fortunately, a study conducted by psychology professor Gail Matthews did take place! And her results concur with the urban myth of the Yale study. In a 1 month period, people with written goals achieved an average 74% of their goals, nearly double that of those who had merely thought about their goals for the coming month.

Now, hands up: how many of you have a plan for your business? No, I don't mean the business plan you had to do for the bank. No, I don't mean the one you did when you first started and then it's been filed somewhere ever since (usually, you'll find it at the bottom of your desk drawer). And yes, I do mean ALL types of organisations and departments and teams. You MUST have a plan to be working toward.

Words of Wisdom...

"**The great thing in this world is not so much where we are. But in what direction are we moving.**" Oliver Wendell Holmes

Plans are often derided because many of them *are* simply done as a tick box exercise: they don't matter and because they don't matter, they don't motivate and because they don't motivate they don't achieve anything. But a business without a plan is like a ship without a wheel: sooner or later you're going to hit the rocks.

FATAL PLANNING

Many of those businesses that do have a REAL Plan also make several common mistakes.

---

[13]. Don't you just love the internet?

The plans are too board room driven. That is, the language of them is high-fluting and pretentious. Too many acronyms and terminologies creep in. Too many graphs. The board room like graphs. It shows the shareholders (or trustees etc) that they understand the complexities of managing the business. And too much of it is focused on telling employees what they should be doing and how they must behave. They are too process-oriented.

They are too ambitious. Listen, how many of you have decided to start from £0 and have a £MILLION turnover within 1 or 2 years? Or to grow your business by 200% and trim costs by 50%? The guy who held the record for the most marathons run in a month didn't decide one day to get up and run a marathon by the end of the week. He started out by running to his nearest lamppost and back on day one. On day two he ran to the second lamppost and back. And so on. To create a sustainable business you must remember that success is about pace and not how fast you can sprint. Which brings us to:

The plans are too short-term. This is a truly western capitalist disease, especially prevalent in the UK and USA. How much is in it for me today? Or how much can we make this quarter? We deal in one year plans. The Chinese and Japanese deal in generational plans. In the long term, all other things remaining equal, what do you think will end up being the biggest and most successful business zone? East or West? The Japanese miracle following the Second World War was due to the fact that they had a plan to improve efficiency and reliability in small incremental steps on a daily basis, and they monitored it daily. Ironically, many of their problems today are due to the picking up of bad habits from the way we do business in the west![14]

Now let me be clear here. I am NOT saying you have to have a 20 year plan in detail. I AM saying you should have a 20 year plan for where you want your company to be, with a detailed plan for year 1, and a framework plan for years 2 & 3. These plans should also be completely

---

[14] Ok, it's more complicated than that, but this remains a major factor.

adaptable because YOU WILL NEED TO MAKE CHANGES. Gone are the times when a market would be stable for 5 years or more, market places aren't particularly stable over a period of a year now. But you must have a clear idea of where you want to go, supported by detailed planning in the short term.

The goals remain goals because they are not expressed in SMART[15] ways. Too often I see goals expressed like this:

"We will become the market leader in widgets by the end of the year."

Or;

"We will improve our widgets so that they are better than anyone else."

SMART as an approach has become derided and is almost always met with rolled eyes and an "oh no, here we go again- we KNOW this stuff" attitude. But knowing something and *DOING* it are two different things. Just look at the two goals above. Questions that instantly spring to mind should be: When? How? What? Why? You must think differently and turn your goals into true objectives.

PLANNING FOR SUCCESS

So, how then should we formulate our plans?

Of course doing the opposite of all the above is a great start, but there are a couple of other tricks of the trade you can do also. The key questions to ask when starting the planning process are what do I want, why do I want it and by when? So long as you keep these questions in your mind and the minds of those working on your plan then the plan will start to shape up quickly and focus on the way forward.

So what should you consider when you are designing your plan?

---

[15] Specific, Measurable, Achievable, Realistic, Timed

Keep it real. Moderate the language; express your objectives and reasons for wanting to achieve those objectives in plain English, but don't be afraid to use emotional words either. The purpose of your plan is not to simply provide a direction and a set of objectives to achieve. It has to give you and everyone else in your organisation the motivation to do it! The language should excite and drive you.

Get it out of the board room. This applies even if you're a small company without a board structure as such, or even if you're the head of a team. Get your staff involved in the planning process. If you're a community group, get your community involved. Have a fun day, play with it, get everyone to buy in and own the plan. That way, everyone feels they have a stake in making the plan a success. Don't fall into the trap of just thinking they should be anyway: being paid to deliver against targets to pay the bills is NOT the same as *wanting* to deliver against the objectives that they're set.

Take a bite...

If you have a plan, take an honest look at it and rate your goals against SMART. Are the specific in nature? What is the date you've set for completion? Are they achievable (e.g. do you have enough resources to do them)? Can they realistically be done? How will you measure what you have achieved should an objective be completed? This last one (the M) is the one that most people forget about- but it's the one that lets you know how well you're doing outside the wider objective, and gives you the juice to move on to the next goal or phase etc.

If you haven't got a plan, start now!!!

Set quick wins. This is important even if you're a one-person band. What do I mean? Well, when you're working with community groups or staff who have been used to working in a certain way (and that includes board members, shareholders and trustees) it's best to factor in the idea of keeping them on side. To do this, plan to achieve some quick wins, and also easily achievable milestones spread over a longer period. Make sure you then celebrate those wins and achievements with said staff (and the other hangers on) because you keep them focused on the fact that you're moving forward and achieving results.

If you're on your own, it's just as important to keep your brain on side. Keep rewarding it with both the positive achievements *AND* a gift for achieving them. Yes, I know it's your brain. That's what it *likes* you to *think*. Trust me, you must reinforce positive pathways in your neural nets to stay motivated and dedicated to success. Your brain is programmed to escape pain far more rigorously than to gain pleasure and will therefore nag at you with its doubts and fears. Get your brain instead to respect pleasure more than it fears failure, so that it starts screaming at you: "You're a success monster! Go do some more success stuff!! Don't worry if it goes wrong, everything else is going right!!!"

Try something else...

Combining your vision with a sustainable plan is a great place to start, but to enhance this process still further, see Principle 8: The Prometheus Principle.

Don't confuse movement with achievement. Now, having said that we should use quick wins to keep everyone moving forward, don't fall into the dreaded TBT. That's the Tick Box Trap folks. The trick here is to create sustainable success[16] and not simply a set of outputs or immediate gratification. Activity without achievement is a distraction, or something you do to relax. So, running a client consultancy day just to say you've done it means you've ticked off the activity box, but what

---

[16] I do not and will not ever simply define success in monetary terms. You should avoid this too. You might well turnover £1m this year but if it means you lost your family and/or your health in the process, what's the point?

was the measurable achievement in terms of real benefits for your business. And no (and I know a very dangerous executive in a local council who thinks this way), adding up how many people attended the event is **NOT** measuring success.

Don't suffocate it. Your Plan should be seen as being alive; a living, breathing creature that will grow and adapt over time. As such you should review its progress, make changes where needed and celebrate when it has been successful. That means it should not be buried at the bottom of a filing cabinet drawer. You need to check in with it, and get your staff (etc) to check in with it at least once a month. I check mine weekly! Think about it- if you check your plan only once a quarter or even a year, how can you keep focused on moving in the right direction? If you check monthly you have 12 x more effectiveness and chances of keeping on course. If you check weekly, it's a whole new ballgame.

Don't let the plan suffocate you. I want to stress this part: too many "consultants" say Plans should be set in stone, that you must achieve the objectives contained therein within the times specified. This is rubbish. Your plan MUST be adaptable. An unexpected guest may appear (see Principle 6: The Unexpected Guest), conditions may change, a fantastic opportunity may arise that needs swift action. If you are simply locked into a plan you will miss these opportunities, or get killed by an unexpected guest, or simply realise that you have a goal to achieve by tomorrow and drop everything to do a rushed job so you can simply tick box it off.

Make it sustainable. Right, you have your plan set up to deliver against this financial year, broken in quarters with monthly sub-targets (or milestones in project speak), so you're ahead of the game, yes? Well, no, not really. It IS important that you have a plan that incorporates this micro-plan (i.e a short term plan) but you MUST think about the future. Your Plan MUST look at where you want to be in 5, 10 and 20 years time. I think it was SONY who had an original plan that looked at what the company wanted to be in a century from when it was formed.

Now, am I saying that you have to do a 20 year plan with set objectives, milestones and monthly SMART targets? Of course not! But if you have a general idea of what you want to achieve long term, and keep adjusting your yearly plans to move you toward this, then do you think your yearly plan will, by default, include more sustainable objectives? You bet it will.

There are many more aspects to consider when making a Plan, but these seven considerations, when applied, will enable you to create a plan that is more rewarding than 99% of your competitors, or increase your chances of success 1000-fold. We can always do advanced planning later if you want to bring someone like me in to run a workshop and planning session.

Coping with indigestion?

Q: **Can having a Plan with easy to achieve objectives and milestones really drive you to success?**

A: *Of course and let me explain how. If you look at the quick wins and easy milestones as course corrections in a journey you'll always be put back on the right path. To illustrate this visually, ask someone to join you in a little experiment. Stand against the wall in a room somewhere. Your colleague is a typical plan stuck in a drawer somewhere. The wall you are standing against is your start point and the wall opposite is your destination 5 years hence. You are where you will be if you have a Plan that is SMARTly organised with many easy steps.*

Now, turn yourself so that you are only angled 5 degrees or so differently from your colleague. Take a step forward and measure where you are in relation to one another. Not much difference is there. Okay, take another step forward and now measure where you are in relation to one another.

Repeat the process until you reach the wall. That small, incremental difference taken at the start of your journey enables you to end up in massively different place doesn't it?

Q: Shouldn't we set objectives that stretch the organisation so that we can grow?

A: *There is absolutely nothing wrong with setting ambitious objectives and targets, none at all. But you MUST make them so that they are achievable and sustainable- don't be like the woodsman and the saw. You don't know this story? Stephen Covey uses it to press a point in his book The 7 Habits of Highly Effective People.*

Here's my version: A woodsman starts sawing down trees, and he sets to at a cracking pace because he has a target of cutting down 25 per day for 5 days because the business he works for has an order that has to be fulfilled by Friday. It's usually a two man job taking four days, but the business also has an objective of reducing costs by 40% over the year so they give the one man an extra day and agree to pay him a bonus if he hits the target.

Pretty soon he's cut down lots of trees but as the week progresses it's getting harder and harder. When he mentions this to a passer by, the passer by suggests that he stops, has a rest and sharpens the saw. The woodcutter pauses for a moment and then snaps back- Can't do that, I've got another 10 trees to cut down today!

The issue with this approach is that it is too narrowly focused on the output. Eventually either he will become too tired or the saw will break from not being properly maintained and the target will be missed. By only doing 20 trees on the Wednesday but taking the time to rest and sharpen the saw be might do 28 for Thursday and 27 for Friday. Stretching is one thing, breaking the machine is another.

5

Play Nice!
Being Macho is a lazy way to manage!

So you're a Type A personality, a go getter who wants to get ahead. You've been promoted to senior management or director level and you've got your sights on going higher still. All you've got to do is whip those whinging employees into shape and bob's your uncle.

There are of course many ways to be an effective manager. You could lead from the front and by example. You could be a visionary leader who enthuses loyalty and respect. You could even be a team player who engenders a feeling of mutual support and respect. So why do so many managers simply behave like bullies?

Here's a story for you that is true; only the names have been changed to protect the guilty. You will probably know this story from your own experiences.

Peter is a driven man. He wants to be the Chief Executive of an organisation. It doesn't really matter which organisation, so long as he can be Chief Executive. He knows the right things to say, and has the skill to know what hot buttons need pressing to get him the maximum political support. He takes on not only the targets set by his masters, but creates hundreds more that can be clearly demonstrated by tick boxes. He then volunteers his department to take on additional duties to tick boxes for his masters. He still says the right things.

His Department start to crank out the results. Box after box is ticked. Things look fantastic in the report. Outputs have never been higher. He gets promoted. His new Department starts to crank out the same increase in outputs. The man is a god. And the proof that he is a great manager is there for all to see because his replacement lower down just doesn't seem to be able to get the same results. Well, not everyone can be as good as our Peter after all.

Peter then moves on to another organisation at a higher level. After all, he says all the right things, knows which hot buttons to press, and can show those 100s of ticked boxes. The process starts again, and after a couple of promotions for being an output god, he moves onto another organisation and repeats the process. After all, he must be a superstar because the organisations he leaves all seem to go into decline several months later. Any organisation would be lucky to have him.

But there is a problem. Peter is a corporate sociopath. He doesn't care about your organisation. He has no regard for your staff, and scant recognition of the needs of your customers. He sees them as nothing but tools to achieve his goals. In the short term, your needs and the needs of your customers coincide with his, but longer term the effects are disastrous.

Once you start to properly analyse the situation you begin to see the truth of the situation. Staff are 3 times more likely to have long term illness under his stewardship. They are left exhausted and demoralised. They do not feel valued or supported by the organisation that they work for. After all, they have been left to the mercy of this sociopath bully and when complaints were raised they were ignored as bleating because look at the results! But even there, it becomes apparent a few months after Peter has moved on that the programmes are unsustainable, that a culture of self-improvement or monitoring is not present, or that simply the resources were never put in place to maintain them.

Words of Wisdom...

"Correction does much but encouragement does more." Goethe.

By the time you realise this, it is too late. Peter has left the organisation or being promoted to such a level you simply cannot fire him. You have to hope someone else makes him an offer he can't refuse. Unfortunately the industry you work in is a small community and the word is out: no one will touch him with a barge pole. You're stuck with him.

Does this sound like it's too far-fetched? It isn't. This is exactly what occurred. I have seen this man reduce people to tears. I have seen him publicly humiliate even senior managers who weren't subservient enough to his ego. And I have seen him leave those who thought he was their friend and mentor to simply take the blame when it goes wrong, leaving them to their fate. And I have seen many more like him.

Why is it that in this country we seem to create these management monsters who think the only way to be manage is to shout louder than anyone else?

The reasons are many and varied but usually distil into a few common and condensed principles.

The first is that we simply don't choose people to be managers for the right reasons. In fact, there's the mistake there. We shouldn't be choosing managers, we should be choosing leaders. But even here, we choose people because they look and sound the part. We don't look any deeper than the smooth and shiny veneer.

More Words of Wisdom...

"The more we know about leadership, the more we understand it is about relationships." Carol Mead, director of community outreach organisation, Canberra, Australia

The second reason is that we don't properly explain what the role of a manager should be, and we most certainly don't provide proper training for the role. So managers fumble along. They think authority comes from the title so instantly bark out orders and expect staff to follow them unquestionably and get frustrated when they don't. I am ashamed to say that in my first supervisory role I acted just like Gareth from The Office. My ego was stroked and I thought management was about control.

It isn't! It's about supporting your team so they can do their job. By doing that you achieve your own targets anyway, but we fail to recognise this because we simply haven't been told how to.

My first true boss, Stephen, was remarkable at this. He trusted you to do the job, didn't assume you knew everything connected to it, but didn't treat you like a child needing constant supervision either. He told you what he needed, some of the potential pitfalls and some potential ladders, and how you then went about it was up to you, with the door open when you needed to query something or ask for help. Unfortunately I didn't work for him long enough the first time to really learn this lesson, hence why I ended up learning the hard way in those early days! Oh and I say my first true boss because my first actual boss was nicknamed Mad Dog- and he was actually proud of that accolade.

A third reason is probably the simplest: it's because that's the way *we* were managed! It's the story of the mom who, at Christmas, would always chop the ends of the pork joint before it went into the oven. Eventually, her children asked her one year why she did it and at first she couldn't think why. Finally she remembered that it was what her mom used to do, but she didn't know why. When they talk to grandma, it turns out that she used to cut the ends off because they only had a small oven! You must stop, ask questions about the history of a way of doing things and then break the mould if necessary.

Another senior executive I encountered was also a mad dog. Let's call him Peter as well. He used to talk about "ripping the face off the competition" and you could literally see the veins on his increasingly purple head starting to throb and stick out. Scary. He used to drop in at branches and point to a salesperson and demand he be taken to one of their customers there and then so he could show them how to sell. It didn't matter what the customer had on that day either.

Take a bite...

As manager, ask yourself these questions: do I support my staff or tell them what to do? Do I deserve or expect respect? Do I trust them to do the job or harass them every step of the way? Be honest with yourself. If you answered in the negative way for any of these, you need to consciously take control of your behaviour and engender change within yourself.

I remember hearing that he was once in front of the management team of a very large bank, doing his rip the face off routine. This bank was not a customer of his company and the account manager had spent nearly a year setting up this appointment with him but Peter insisted that he not only go along, but that he take the lead in the presentation and discussion.

Unfortunately Peter extended his rant to include the poor vision of this management team for working with the competitor instead of going with his company in the first place. The rant continued. His head became prune shaped.

The senior executive of the bank called security.

After this, whenever Peter went in search of his random "take me to your leader" trips, the sales people had told all their reception staff to warn them he was on his way, so whilst he went into the department through one route, they would disembark en-mass via another. It was only toward the end of his secondment to the UK operations that he started to adopt a softer approach, but by that time it was too late.

So what's the answer?

Simply change your focus. Become a manager who supports their team or organisation. Don't micro manage. Trust more. If it goes wrong, don't sack everyone and make them feel like failures. Learn the lesson about the failure and improve the systems, processes or skills where necessary. Above all, stop being macho. In the end you'll destroy everything you're working so hard to achieve.

Try something else...

Okay, so you need to change your approach and create a better management style and productive working arrangement with your staff. See the next chapter, Walk The Talk, for more distinctions on how you can do this.

Coping with indigestion?

Q: Okay, I get that there's a better way of doing things, but to be honest, I have been that micro-manager and control freak. I want to change but my staff think I'm a jerk- how can I get them onside?

A: It won't be easy. You could start by being honest, showing them that you read this book and it has made you realise that you haven't covered yourself in glory as a manager. Then outline *that you intend now to change the way you do things. You won't be perfect, and you will still expect them to do their job, but you will also try harder to let them do it, and only be involved when they ask for help or advice.*

Q: **But if I just learn to trust that they'll do the job won't they take the piss and drop me in it?**

A: *I am not saying for a moment that you absolve yourself of responsibility for what you, your team or company has to achieve. And yes, there will be members of staff that try to take advantage. But you're the one in charge, it's up to you to recognise who needs micro-managing (or dispensing with if needs be) and who you can trust, with some initial direction, to simply get on with the job. I am not suggesting for a moment that you become everyone's best friend, just that you become more human.*

6

Walk The Talk!

How can you expect others to use your products if you don't.

Walk into Microsoft offices and you won't see LINUX servers or Apple iMACs (save in the Office development team's, er, offices). Why? Because *they* want to be the intelligence that drives the computing environment.

You know how it goes. There you are, promoting yourself as being the top guru in time management services. You've even created a time management product that you sell over the web or at workshops. And then someone sees that you're using someone else's time management product!

And no, I'm not talking about myself. I don't sell TM products, I sell strategies and distinctions to help you maximise any time management product you currently use. But enough selling, let's get to the nub of what I'm talking about here.

Walking the talk is one of those great clichéd expressions that we've all heard of, but then pay scant regard to. In our heads, we think about scenarios like the above one with Microsoft, or how, if you're CEO at Ford Motors it would be a bad thing to turn up to work in a Mercedes

Benz. But the concept goes way deeper than that. Walking the talk MUST extend to two other areas; your service usage, that is aligning your usage of services with what you promote; and yourself- that is, how you behave.

SERVING THE GREATER GOOD

Let's examine what I mean here. Let's say you work for environmental services at a council, in the enforcement team. Your job is to go round warning businesses when they clearly breach environmental legislation or individuals when they fail to use the recycling bins properly, e.g. putting a broken desktop computer in the green bin for garden waste.

Would you then take your car for servicing at a local garage knowing that, whilst not in strict breach of environmental policy, they are pretty morally lax in the area? Even if they are cheap, you can't do that (or shouldn't do it) because it conflicts with the service you are providing.

Words of Wisdom...

"Walking your talk is a great way to motivate yourself. No one likes to live a lie. Be honest with yourself, and you will find the motivation to do what you advise others to do." Vince Poscente

Likewise, being that same person, would it be right for you to spend all day pursuing the council's environmental policy (and enforcing it when necessary) but then go to bed each night leaving the TV on standby, or throwing broken electrical items into the general waste bin instead of taking them to the recycling depot? Again, you shouldn't be doing this because it conflicts with what you do.

Now, don't get me wrong. I am not one to promote the idea that we, as individuals, should be defined by what we do in our job. In fact oft times it's good to forget about what we do when we're in our personal lives;

the lawyer who comes home and starts cross-examining their spouse or kids and then wonders why the family prefer it when they're at work is a good example. You are not a lawyer, you work in law!

No, this is subtly different. What I'm talking about here is avoiding doing things that conflict with your working identity. Think about it in these terms; if you work in the Peace Corp would you be an extra in a promo for a video war game? You might play video games and enjoy Battlefield 3001, but would you go so far as to publicly be seen promoting it? I think not.

And yet so many of us have a day job and then buy in services from competing companies, or act in a way at home that is in direct contradiction to the day job. Bouncers go out and get into a drunken brawl. Police officers cheat on their tax returns. Politicians cheat on their spouses. Directors at computer companies buy a competitors computer for their kids. And so on.

Take a bite...

Right now, take a look around your home and make an audit of all the products or behaviours that you have or do that in some way conflict with your job. For example, if you work at SONY, does your family have a XBOX console, a Panasonic TV or a Toshiba DVD player? If you work for Virgin Airlines are you and your family taking a trip on BA? Add them all up and assess the scale between 1 and 10 (1 is ok, 10 is won't ever be able to leave the house) about how much of a potential embarrassment it would be for your boss or major shareholder to come visiting.

Don't get me wrong. I am not saying that you should go through your house and change absolutely everything. In the SONY example in the Take a Bite box above, your son or daughter may well have the XBOX console because maybe there is a great game on that console that isn't available on the SONY Playstation. But you had also better have a

Playstation in the household too. And the higher up the management ladder you are, the more you had better be standardised on your company's products or services.

WHY IS IT IMPORTANT?

It's important because identity is important. If you work at XYZ Bank but you use ABC Banking services, especially when you are at executive level, then how can you congruently promote your banks services? You can't. You can bluff, and you can bluster, and you can pretend, and for a long time you may get away with it. But sooner or later someone is going to ask; do you use your bank's services?

As embarrassing as that would be, imagine then if it's a reporter on national TV asking the question.

It is important for another reason too. It enables you to understand the workings of your company's products or services so you can be better prepared for questions from clients, prospects or droppers in. Furthermore, it enables you to start to identify weaknesses in the product or service so you can start to feed in incremental improvements.

In effect, it enables you to gain competitive advantage.

Try something else...

Okay, so you're walking the talk and you feel more connected to your organisation. What next? See Focus Area 10, Run a Social Club, for more distinctions on how you can improve your connection to what you do.

There's one final reason why it is important to walk the talk. It gives you an emotional stake in your organisation's success. You start to identify with it and once you do that, your subconscious is programmed to start looking for opportunities, ways to improve, or ways to promote your organisation. And not just you. Imagine your entire workforce being switched on to your organisational success. Wouldn't that be incredible?

Be Your Product

I've concentrated on using physical products and services so far because that's the easiest way to draw examples. However, let's say you are your company's product. For example, The Inform Group doesn't sell physical products, but rather a set of interconnected services: time management skills, presentation skills, business development, goal setting workshops, project management and science & technology workshops to name a few- all based on the ideas in this book.

Within these, I teach various strategies, techniques and distinctions that you, as a client, can use to improve your personal abilities, or the ability of your organisation as a whole. These various tools have been distilled from various sources over the decades (ranging from Tony Robbins, Rob Parsons, Chuck Hughes, Stephen Covey through to PRINCE2 training, IBM Sales Training, Police Investigation Training, CertEd course through to, of course, my own experiences and thinking) and all I do is promote the lessons that have worked for me, and that I have seen work for others after training they have had from me.

The key words in that paragraph are "that have worked for me". For example, I promote the concept of constant improvement and, linked to this, I tell people to learn something new every day. Once I've stood up and delivered a workshop where these concepts are embedded, do I just go home, put the TV on and forget about it?

Absolutely not. I use a technique learned doing my PTTLS and Cert Ed called reflection, where I review what I did, what went well, what didn't go so well, and make changes to that course accordingly. Do I use the time management strategies I promote in workshops to my clients? You bet I do. To the point where my ex-wife thought I was obsessed. Yet think about this. In the last couple of years I have had to manage a return to health, develop my business, complete a CERT ED, write several books, work on my BSc, provide an environment where my children feel loved and completely supported, be a good friend and a loving partner, work on a new comic book venture AND organise and run two weekly radio shows, and other specials, as well as develop a radio station[17]. Do you think that I could even teach someone else's time management course? Wouldn't it be better to base everything on what I do? Wouldn't it be more passionate? Wouldn't I be better prepared to answer difficult questions?

I think you know the answers. I fully utilise ALL the techniques I talk and train about, whether they are original creations of mine, adaptations of others, or simply the concepts of other people (giving full credit where necessary).

What you must do is the same.

Coping with indigestion?

Q: I've done the audit and my house is full of competitive products. Do I have to junk them all?

A: *That depends on your position within the company. Certainly, primary offerings should be replaced. Do it over a time that suits your budget of course, but get started straight away.*

Q: I've done the audit and I use competitive services but they're better than those the company I work for provide. What do I do?

A: *Start looking for another job. I don't mean to be glib but if you really believe that then you're creating an internal conflict that ends up making you feel miserable. You can't be truly effective at your workplace, even if you're someone who likes to give their all.*

---

[17] Crossfire Radio- see www.crossfireradio.net

7
Everyone Works in Sales!
Yes, that means you!

There's a divide in many organisations. You either work in sales or you don't. Management sometimes even encourage this kind of thinking and ask the non-sales departments to make allowances for the sales department. After all, they're the ones that pay your wages aren't they?

Most organisations fail to realise that there is one true axiom in business: the best sales people in the world cannot compete against the business that has everyone selling for it!

Just about all the businesses that have a direct sales need[18] fall into the trap of viewing their sales people as somehow separate from the rest of the business. Whether this comes from the management culture, organisational structure or the beliefs of the different departments is irrelevant because it damages your business either way.

But this concept also extends to a far wider audience. If at the moment you're reading this thinking, "oh, we're a public sector organisation, we

---

[18] I mean here any business that has to sell product or service to generate revenues, whether direct to consumers or from business to business.

don't do sales so this chapter isn't relevant to me" let me assure you of this; you are dead wrong.

Lesson one here is this: EVERY ORGANISATION, WHETHER PRIVATE OR PUBLIC, REVENUE EARNING OR NOT, <u>MUST</u> SELL ITSELF AT EVERY OPPORTUNITY.

If you run a council department, or a 3rd sector housing management project, or provide free food for the homeless, you must still sell what you are and what you do to someone, whether it's the local authority who will support your activity, the community you work in who will use what you provide, or the (increasingly hard to find) funding agency who will issue you with a grant to continue delivering your service. The principles I am going to discuss in this chapter are just as applicable even if you don't have a team of sales individuals.

Words of Wisdom...

"We must all hang together, or assuredly, we shall all hang separately." - Benjamin Franklin

The issue with how we look at private businesses and public sector services as being different is incredibly destructive because it creates belief systems that everything must behave in a certain perceived way. Any deviation from the perceived view meets with suspicion and even derision. And it is in the concept of selling that we have the most narrow belief system of all.

PUBLIC OR PRIVATE: YOU ARE ALL SALES PEOPLE.

Now, I can hear "proper" sales people really moaning that it takes skills and certain attitudes to be a sales person and of course you're right- if you adhere to the narrow definition of what a sales person is.

Let me explain. Working *in* sales is a difficult job. You have to have a self-belief that verges on arrogance. You have to have a certain gift of the gab. You need to know psychology, how to present or communicate, and have strong intuition skills. The best sales people are also incredibly empathic and understand that you sell to the solution that meets the intellectual needs and the emotional wants of the customer. You must also have skin like a rhinoceros. In this strict definition of the role of sales person, I am most certainly not a sales man. The thought of cold calling leaves *me* cold.

But here's the rub. If I don't sell what I do, then my business doesn't make money. If your special investigation unit doesn't sell what it achieves, then the council will shut it down to make cuts. If your community group doesn't sell the impact it has on the wellbeing of the local community the funding agency won't issue you with another grant.

Take a bite...

At random, stop members of your team and ask them to list five things they love about working for you. Then ask them to list 5 things you could do better. Do NOT argue with them or make them wrong (or retrospectively punish them later). Look carefully at both lists and act on them. Improve and promote what you're doing right (especially if they appear more than once), and look to make changes where you're not so good (ditto). Then REWARD people if their suggestions for improvement really make a difference.

So here is Lesson Two: YOU ALL WORK IN SALES.

In private companies with a selling arm this distinction is even more lost in the hustle and bustle of daily business needs and structural precepts. There is the sales department, full of those smartly dressed men and women who breeze in with their smooth attitudes, smooth skin and smooth hair; and there are the accountancy department, warehousing, marketing department and board etc who help the salespeople sell.

But we fail to understand that to really maximise the selling power of your sales team, or rather the revenue earning power of your sales team, then everyone else must be selling your business as well. It's not enough to say that warehousing got the orders out on time, or the accountancy department did a special arrangement with a new customer or that marketing generated a new lead. What you have to realise is that one bad word in the wrong ear from any employee could cost that sale you've been working on for months. Even if the bad word is about the sales person.

I am not saying that you should send everyone on a sales training course (most of them are rubbish anyway, I should know I've sat through dozens in my time) but you should have a workshop, at the very least annually, where you talk all employees through the following:

1. **Everyone is in sales within your organisation.** They should be listening out for opportunities to bring into the company, and they should be rewarded if the opportunity is valid.
2. **Careless talk costs lives.** In this instance, carelessly slagging[19] off the company in a pub could be overheard by the customer your organisation is in negotiations with. Every time that happens (and trust me, it does) you put financial pressure on the company, which could end up costing jobs. Maybe even yours.
3. **The main positives about your company and its offerings.** You'll be amazed how often members of your staff- at every level- don't know diddlysquat about your main products or services. They simply turn up for their salary (or pay check for our US cousins) and don't feel any connection with the company they work for.

---

[19] UK slang for criticising something with particular loudness.

Now, this last point is critical for the managers and executives to appreciate. If your employees don't feel they have a connection with your company then you are the ones doing something wrong. You either haven't created a culture where employees feel valued and respected, or you haven't put in place a significant enough induction or training programme to get them to feel that they truly know what they are doing and why (in relation to the success of the business) they are doing it.

Try something else...

We've talked about making your employees feel valued and able to bring in opportunities for your organisation. See Principle 5: The Round Table Principle for a strategy that can help you do this.

In the end, it comes down to this: do you want every single person in your organisation praising what your organisation does or not?

Coping with indigestion?

Q: If I find people are being negative all the time should I fire them?

A: *If they are being publicly negative time after time then yes. You should of course first try to find out what the issues are and move on them, but if it continues then you don't really have a choice.*

8

Waste Not Want Not!

If you don't want the pain of cutting, don't bloat in the first place!

Things are going well. In fact, they're brilliant, so you decide to upgrade everyone's IT systems, get nicer company cars, and hire more staff. There's nothing inherently wrong with this but did you stop and ask: can I pay for all this if times go bad?

In my personal life I'm a nightmare for bloating. See that DVD boxset at only a tenner? I'd better get it now whilst it's so cheap! I mean, it's only a tenner and I have £15 in my pocket after all. Forget for the moment that I still have 50 DVDs yet to watch. Imagine now if I extended that principle to running my business. Yet we can all fall into that very trap!

There is an economic cycle. Things go up, they go down. Times are good, then not so good. Boom and bust however is not part of the cycle. Boom and bust is the consequence of how we, as companies, governments and individuals behave *during* those cycles.

When times are good, greed sets in. We inflate our salaries or bonuses, improve the company car scheme, set about increasing staff levels to cope with the new levels of business, move to a more prestigious part of the city, bring in those expensive consultants to recommend the best IT system and jump in to install the new big thing before the competition. Why? Because times are good and we can afford to do it.

Except we can't.

Because the cycle will turn into a negative and there is a certain scientific principle that applies to every aspect of life whether we accept it or not: For every action, there is an equal and opposite reaction[20].

In other words, as much as you have bloated your company during the good times, you will now have to go on an extremely costly diet, not just in terms of affecting your competitiveness and profit margins, but in terms of the human cost of lost jobs. You only have to look around at the devastation caused by the recent banking crisis, the effects of which are still being felt as I write this, to see the truth of what I say (although many bankers *STILL* haven't learned this simple tenet!).

Words of Wisdom...

"At that time a senator who was on the Joint Committee of Atomic Energy said rather quietly, 'You know, we're having a little problem with waste these days.' I didn't know what he meant then, but I know now." David R. Brower

WE HAVE TO ATTRACT THE BEST TALENT

There are several arguments put forward as to why we should inflate everything to do with our business. Chief amongst them is the heading

---

[20] Newton's Third Law of Motion

of this section. But there is also the idea that extra staff are needed to support the growing business, new IT systems are a must to support the extra staff and we should reward our existing staff because we have been so successful over the last few years, so isn't a new car scheme a good idea?

Let's take these one at a time.

The idea that we have to attract the best staff is the excuse given by every big business whether it's banking, supermarkets, councils, NHS trusts or consultancy firms. It's the justification that is used to justify the huge bonuses still being paid out to executives and the average 50% hike in executive pay whilst most lower paid employees were forced to take a pay cut (a pay freeze folks is effectively a cut as well)[21]. The argument goes like this: if we don't pay these huge amounts to our executives they will go to another company. To frighten off Government legislation they even promote the idea that these executives would go to other countries.

Yet this justification misses one truly thundering point: it was the so-called best talent that caused the latest economic disaster in the first place.

It also promotes the idea that there is no inherent loyalty to a company at the executive level, and completely ignores the mountain of research that shows that people, especially with families, with some exceptions, will not give up their country to go live and work in foreign climes.

Now, I don't know about you but I would want people working for me, at any level, to want to work for me. I want them to buy into the ethos of what I am trying to achieve with my company. In return I will give them a good basic remuneration. Rewards would be ad hoc and at my discretion. If they simply want more money, then they can go with my blessing because they have failed to see what I am trying to build. True enough, as my revenues and profits increase, the people who are with

---

[21] As I write, the world is still in the recession caused by the greed of our banks

me from the start will see their rewards also increase, but the culture of my business is also part of the reward. We work in a culture of fun, support and contribution. To me that is more important than what company car I can afford to give them.

I therefore point this out in interviews. I want people who get excited by the prospect of contributing to the greater good as part of their day job, who love the idea of coming to a place of work where they can have fun and feel valued. When people ask what the benefits are, I tell them and watch their reactions when they realise it's not a BMW or annual bonus worth 50% of their salary.

When hiring your staff you must also learn to ask the question: is this person going to deliver long term benefits for the business or are they here simply for the financial package?

The next trap we fall into during good times, is hiring new staff to cope with the work levels. There are times when this is imperative, true enough. But all too often it is the lazy approach to managing a business. Operations are struggling with demand, hire new warehousing staff! Sales can't cope with the leads coming in, hire new sales people! IT systems are at breaking point, hire new technicians! Oh bugger, I can't cope with all these new reportees, so put in place a new tier of management!

Now, there are times when adding to headcount should definitely be a course of action, but first of all you should ask the following questions:

1. Can we improve the management systems and physical processes to help cope with the demands on operations/sales/IT/etc?
2. Is this rise in demand a permanent truth or a temporary market effect? For example, is it the end of the financial year, or have you just done a hugely successful campaign tied into a one-off event such as London 2012?

3. What level of staff do we need to hire? For example, to assist the sales team handle their leads, do we need more salespeople (at top recruitment and payment fees) or would sales assistants (at a lower payment structure) suffice?
4. What will be the structural effect and costs of hiring these new members of staff? Will I need new managers or supervisors?
5. Can I afford all these overheads if the market declines? If not, are there temporary solutions I can put in place? For example, temporary staff.

Now, some consultants will argue that if you don't keep things running smoothly then you affect your business profitability anyway, and they are right. But how much of a delay can it cost to ask and answer those 5 questions?

Take a bite...

Look at your existing systems and processes and properly analyse what's working and what isn't. Look for ways to improve their performance and resilience. Get feedback from staff (or family members if just starting out) and customers (or service users if public service). If necessary organise a competition for best suggestion on how to improve performance. Start with the most mission critical process, and work down the list.

The next area is around getting those top IT consultants and systems to maintain competitive advantage. Competitive advantage is a must, but to get it must you have the best, most expensive IT systems in place? I am picking on IT systems here but this is true of any tool or equipment you need for your business. The questions you must ask here are:

1. Is what I have fit for purpose?
2. How much competitive advantage will it give me if I put the ZEDCORP3000 system in place?

3. What is the cost/benefit ratio of installing this system?
4. WHO IS IT I AM COMPETING AGAINST? The ZEDCORP3000 might give you a competitive edge over Microsoft, but what if you only need to compete against Joe Bloggs Computing Ltd? Can you really justify the cost on that basis?

BRINGING IT TOGETHER

To bring this section to a close I want to tell you a joke that was told at a conference I was helping stage manage, by an American Marketing Director called Glenn Miller. Yes, we did all the swing jokes too, but listen up because I never forgot what he had to say.

He started his talk to an audience of business executives thus:

Two men are walking through the jungle when suddenly a great big lion jumps out at them, roaring in clear hunger and anticipation of a nice fleshy dinner. One of the men starts running around in circles in a blind panic, screaming, "We're going to die! We're going to die!" The other man however, calmly takes off his hiking boots, reaches into his rucksack, pulls out a pair of sneakers and starts to put them on. The first man notices what he is doing and screams at him- "What are you doing?! Are you mad!?! You can't out run a lion!!!" The second man, standing, looks up and says quietly: "I don't need to out run the lion, I only need to out run you."

The lesson here is this.

Growth is good, in fact it's necessary because if you're not growing you're dying. There is no standing still. But you must grow organically. To do that, look only at your nearest competitors and prepare your growth plans on gaining competitive edge over them. Spend only what you need to pull away from them where process changes, improvements in marketing or tweaks in product or service design aren't enough.

Then look at the next level up, and make your plans accordingly.

By doing this, when the bad times come, you won't have bloated. You'll be trim and elegant, and faster on the move. Whilst your competitors are busy cutting and slashing and downsizing to survive, you'll be focused on chasing the remaining opportunities that exist to see you through to the next cycle of good times.

Try something else...

For more thinking on avoiding pain for your organisation, see Principle 1: The Caduceus Principle for other strategies that can help you do this.

Coping with indigestion?

Q: You say I should focus on my nearest competitors yet I've always been told to go after the biggest and best! Which is right?

A: *You should of course always look to compare yourself with the market leader in your industry. If nothing else you can look at what they have done to get where they are (including what they did wrong so you can avoid the same mistakes!). Furthermore, the more you can get your employees and clients thinking about you in the same breath as your market leader, the more you punch above your weight in that marketplace. Perception is king as they say.*

However, don't confuse speed of growth and market share with sustainable success. Plan to rise through the ranks (of competitors) one level at a time, that way you expand your company and resources organically and not in one great big junk food banquet which leaves you feeling satisfied in the moment, but in reality leaves you bloated and empty when the effect wears off.

9
Be a Marketing Magician!
Do more with what you have!

That marketing consultant has come to your business with a 12 point plan to achieve market dominance and wants to charge you £100,000 for the work. But wait, do you really need to spend £100k, even if business is going well?

The consultants say you've got to use the internet! Most of us are fully aware of what the internet is and what it can do, but equally, often it sounds like an area where you need to be a master of black arts! SEO! Social Media! Search rankings! Podcasts! Quick, get me a consultant to do all this for me. The problem is that most consultants want you to subscribe to the theory that they are magicians, when instead with a little practice, we can do the tricks ourselves.

You too can be a marketing magician. And it needn't cost a fortune either. There are two principles you need to know about marketing before you start.

1. **Everything must be integrated.**
2. **You must market what your client needs, not what you want to sell.**

That's it. No, really, this is all you need to be aware of to really restructure your sales and marketing activities so that you gradually, organically increase revenues and profits without spending almost as much in time and resources as the extra that you've earned.

So, let's look at these two principles in a bit more detail.

EVERYTHING MUST BE INTEGRATED

There's no doubt that the internet is a fantastic marketing tool that can bring huge benefits to the revenue potential of any business. When used correctly, it is also a great leveller. That's how very small organisations can compete with huge multinational companies: you simply have a better web presence that enables you to punch way above your weight.

However, there's a little problem with the internet: you can be the best organisation in your market, you can have the greatest products and services in the world. But if no-one knows you are there, then you will fail.

Ah, I hear you ask, but won't we come up when people do a search for our kind of product or service? Y'know, if they Google it?

No. Search engines don't work like that. Now, I don't intend to do an in-depth discussion on search engine technologies and algorithms because the fact is, they are always changing the rules. If you're reading this book a year from when I write it, such a discussion will be out of date.

However, it is useful for you to understand the basic ways they work so you can get started changing the way you use your website now.

Words of Wisdom...

"If you don't believe in your product, or if you're not consistent and regular in the way you promote it, the odds of succeeding go way down. The primary function of the marketing plan is to ensure that you have the resources and the wherewithal to do what it takes to make your product work." Jay Levinson

First off, I need to come back to the idea of people not knowing you are on the internet. You see, to listen to many consultants, the internet is the holy grail of marketing and PR and, eventually, selling. The fact is that the internet used on its own cannot deliver any real benefit.

So, lesson one: EVERYTHING YOU DO ON THE INTERNET MUST BE REFLECTED IN YOUR TRADITIONAL MARKETING MATERIALS AND VICE VERSA.

That also means that every traditional marketing tool you use, from brochures, leaflets, adverts, business cards (yes business cards are a marketing tool), van signs, office signs, letters, emails and radio adverts etc, MUST HAVE YOUR WEBSITE ADDRESS, and if you have Facebook, Linkedin or Twitter accounts those too, INCLUDED SOMEWHERE WITHIN IT.

By doing this, you start to drive people to use your website. And the more they use it, the more you can use your site to push offers and services that they need. To further maximise the effect, whenever you launch some activity on the web, make sure that your paper based or email based activity supports that launch- drive people to that specific web address. And use your website to promote traditional marketing activity also, for example if you are running a sales conference, use the website to push the event, and assist visitors by enabling them to book a place online.

Take a bite...

Review all your existing paper products- business cards, brochures, adverts, letters, signs etc, plus your email templates. Do they have your website address? If you have Twitter, Facebook, LinkedIn etc, are they clearly labelled too? If not, scrap as many of them as you can afford to and change them TODAY. Make sure that new templates are prepared with these details for when items are due for reprints.

Right, I promised a quick discussion on search engines. Search engines use something called "rankings" to position results when a search is done. It used to be that the more hits you had the higher up the ranking you were. Then Google and Yahoo etc introduced the idea of relevancy to the algorithms. In basic terms if you search for "manufacturers of widgets", the results don't just bring up websites that have the word manufacturer and widgets on them, they look for associated terms.

This gave rise to the so called science of Search Engine Optimisation (SEO), for which some consultancy firms charged a fortune to embed certain words and phrases (often invisible to the naked eye) so that your site appeared high in the search results. The truth is however, that being clever with the use of words on your site does not require you spending £15,000-£100,000 on a web development agency to add SEO to your site. Google for example, provide you with tools that enable you to see what kind of information you should provide to match up with certain search phrases.

Now you'll notice I said "information" to provide, not what words you use. The search engine providers wised up the tricks being pulled so extended the algorithms to really analyse the kind of materials on your website- even video and audio content- that support your use of key words.

But again, you can manage that without paying thousands of pounds.

Now, am I saying that web developers are superfluous to business need? Absolutely not. I know basic web design, I can do web analysis, but I am NOT a web designer. A proper web designer can bring out some wonderful tools, concepts and strategies that are real tricks of the trade. But you MUST also learn enough about web design to make sure that the website you end up with is fit for purpose, that it doesn't just look great but also delivers what you need it to deliver to serve the needs of your clients. You can find ideas, free papers and links to other people's free papers on web design and marketing on my site www.darreninform.com to get you started, and you must research web design principles and properly define what you want *before* you bring in any web consultant.

MARKET WHAT YOUR CLIENT NEEDS AND NOT WHAT YOU WANT TO SELL

Another basic principle that even experienced marketers often forget, is that even the best product in the world only has so many people interested in buying it at any one time. In fact studies show that in a room of 100 people that are a target audience for what you have to sell, only 3 of them will want to buy it right now[22].

More Words of Wisdom...

"At any given time, 3% of your prospects are currently in the market to buy your product or service." Chet Holmes

---

[22] Conducted by Business Breakthroughs

The same research shows that, on average, 6-7% are open to buy but not actively looking. That means 90% of people are either not thinking about buying, think they're not interested in what you have to offer or KNOW they're not interested in what you have to offer.

So the question becomes not how many widgets can I sell today but how do I change the interest level of those people who think they don't need my widgets.

Once you approach the marketing plan with this question in mind, your strategies start to move more in the right direction. But you need to add something else into the mix to truly maximise your marketing efforts, and it's one that seems counter intuitive. Don't sell your product or service. Instead, give away education that helps your prospect improve their efficiency, bottom line, success, costs and so on.

What do I mean?

Okay, well, let's say you work in the automobile industry as a car reseller. You have over the years built up a great mailing list, but sales are slow, those Car People have muscled in on the surrounding area and you're feeling the pinch. It's not too bad at the moment, but there is a definite slope off in visitors to your compound. Do you therefore do a blanket mail shot to your database promoting your latest models?

Well, you could do but isn't that what The Car People will be doing too? After all, you've got 3% in need of a car at anyone time, so those 3% get two leaflets, one from you promoting 20 cars from a total of 150, and one from The Car People promoting from over 500 cars. Which one would your prospect most likely go visit on Saturday?

So what if you did something else instead? What if you sent a letter full of performance tips for car owners? And then a week later, a letter with safety tips (this is great of course if you can tie the theme in with a local or national news story)? And then the week after that a fun story about a car failure somewhere in Europe? And then the week after that top tips for choosing a car?

Now, I can almost hear some of you saying that we have a monthly or quarterly newsletter that has this kind of feature in it. But that's not timely, and it's certainly not noticed as much as a letter arriving saying in big bold letters- "THE TOP 10 TIPS FOR BUYING A NEW CAR". Follow that up with "TOP TEN REASONS WHY OLDER CARS FAIL- AND WHAT TO DO ABOUT THEM". But you don't do a hard sale.

Eventually of course you will need to sell, so let's imagine you are going to run an open day showing you how to maintain your car without being a mechanic, handing out canopies and a drink whilst giving really useful information for all visitors.

When they get there, you have an offer running that says you will give a special 33% off for the first 10 buyers for that week. Obviously you don't just launch straight into the offer and you don't spend more than 5-10% of their time pushing it either.

This is called education based selling and it is proving to be very successful. It's why many consultants now give away free lots of useful information on their websites and in blogs. I do the same. I want my clients to feel that they get a huge amount of useful material from me so that when they do need to buy a paper or training session from me, they have already justified the spend.

Try something else...

For more thinking on changing the way you engage with clients and prospects, see Principle 12: The 99 Monkeys Principle for other strategies that can help you do this.

Now, Chet Holmes[23], one of the world's most successful sales people, has a book out called The Ultimate Sales Machine which discusses

---

[23] Chet sadly died recently from a long illness at far too young an age.

education based selling in great detail- you can get it from Amazon- so I'm not going to labour the point here when he does it so much more masterly, but note the key principle is that you shouldn't just do a one off mail shot. It must be a pre-planned, weekly campaign that plays to the needs, wants or fears of your prospects.

Or you could just hire me to do a half day workshop with you and key staff to structure the campaign for you and come up with the key messages. I want to insert a smiley face here but I'm told that's not the done thing in a book.

In conclusion then, remember being a marketing magician basically means getting more out of what you have, or adding new activity (spells!) without laying out a small fortune because you've already put some time into researching and defining what you want.

Coping with indigestion?

Q: Ok, so we've said you must integrate all your marketing activities, and driving everyone to your website is a good idea. But is that all there is to it? What if my company doesn't do much paper based activity?

A: As I said the discussion of how search engines work within this book is only very basic (and they could well have evolved still further by now) and you'll find a wealth of material on my website to give you further detailed distinctions.

However, there are several other quick, easy and (virtually) free steps you can take to help both drive people to your website and get noticed by the "web-crawlers" of search engine providers:

1. Blog. Add a blog to your website and update it regularly. Give your blog a personality and make it useful to your clients wherever possible. Or funny. Or controversial. But don't make it dull.

2. Guest blog. Find other BLOGGERs looking for guest articles and blogs, making sure you include your email, contact details and web site address at the end of the blog. Web-crawlers love to follow links from one website to another.
3. Find complimentary service providers and do a joint-link deal. If you sell cars for example, why not approach a local insurance firm (especially if they are local and not a bank owned service) and offer to promote their service if they let you leave leaflets in their offices and have a link on their website.
4. Update regularly, especially your home page. Web-crawlers notice change.
5. Add relevant information about the market you are in. If you work in electrics you could add energy saving advice, the latest paper on electro-magnetic breakthroughs and the kind of products that might be here in 10 years time, and so on. Remember the web-crawlers look for relevancy.
6. Add audio and video. You don't need an expensive studio to make multimedia blogs. I record my VoiceWORKS audio blogs using my laptop, audioboo and a £5 headset microphone.
7. Add social media activity to your marketing plan: tools such as Twitter, Facebook and LinkedIN (or Manta etc) pages really help your web strategies deliver messages to a wider audience and add connector buttons to all of them. For example, when I update Twitter it automatically shows on my company website (you can follow me at @darreninform). Likewise, a Facebook entry shows up on my Twitter account and on my website.

There's more I could tell you but I don't want to turn this book into one about web marketing. The key thing is connect everything to everything else.

PS I am NOT saying you shouldn't hire web designers- just make sure you are very clear about your needs and strategies and manage them!

10
Run a Social Club!
Not a sweatshop!

How many times do you hear people say: "There can't be much work going on here with all the talking"? Do you say it yourself? If you do, why do you?

The fact is that we spend almost half of our waking hours in a work environment! If we're not enjoying the time then we're going to be miserable. And if we're miserable then we're hardly likely to be very productive are we?

It never ceases to amaze me how many managers fail to understand a very simple premise: a happy worker is a productive worker.

Now, as you will see in arguments elsewhere in this book, various blogs and other rants, I'm not a fan of focusing on "productivity" as a measure of personal, departmental or organisational success. But it is the language that many of you reading this book will understand so for the moment I will use the principle of productivity to explain why having a happy team is a good idea.

There are a number of very basic concepts that fold into the idea of enabling your workforce to be happy, and you probably know most of them. But the question is then: do you actually apply them? As I have said before and will say again, there is a huge difference between knowing something and doing something.

So, what are these basic concepts?

Don't confuse movement with action. Very often the culture of an organisation drives people to making sure they *look* busy. They've learned from experience that if they aren't walking around with boxes of files, or dashing from one meeting room to another, or answering emails by the dozen, then they are viewed as non-productive, or not committed or just plain lazy. That's because we have executives who confuse motion with productivity. It's just plain wrong. You need to alter the definition to the idea below.

Movement without purpose leads to a retreat from productivity. All these people dashing about do so with one purpose: to *look* busy. But being busy does not mean being productive. The amount of energy and time needed to look busy is time and energy taken *away* from generating real productive outputs.

Words of Wisdom...

"Entrepreneurs have a great ability to create change, be flexible, build companies and cultivate the kind of work environment in which they want to work." *Tory Burch*

So the question becomes: why do people do this?

Well, whilst it is true that some people hide behind movement to mask their lack of direction, commitment or ability to contribute, the sad fact is the majority of people do this because the management team expects them to look busy. It is the equivalent of concentrating on ticking boxes on a form rather than delivering real benefits across the board.

In other words, it is the leadership that is at fault, not the activity of those being led.

Let's go back to some more of these concepts.

There is no "I" in team. If you have a team working together, you need them to be working together otherwise there is also no "f" in point[24]. The best way to do that is for the team to know and understand each other. No, I don't mean what grade are they on, or what their job title is. They need to know who they are working with. Their skills and experiences are important, true, but also their plans, their favourite music, what they watch on TV, where they are going on holiday. I'm not saying they need to know their colleagues life history, but chatting whilst working, or making a coffee, goes a long way in helping people understand and bond with other members in their team.

A committed worker is a productive worker. This is true but this concept has been corrupted into meaning that the worker should be answering emails at 11pm at night, or coming in early or staying late, even when there is no real reason for them to do so. Staying there is seen by management as being committed. It misses the wider reality: the worker doesn't refresh, doesn't take a proper rest, doesn't have a laugh with friends and family and therefore becomes less effective at work, simply because their energy is being sapped, or their brain hasn't had a chance to reboot. It goes back **to the idea of sharpening the saw!**

Furthermore, they strive to "appear" committed, they do what's expected of them or what they think conveys commitment. And all the time resenting that they have to do it, with the knock on event that they start to actively look for ways that they can "stick it" to the boss. Longer term, everyone loses.

So we need to change the focus here. A worker is *truly* committed to your organisation when they feel supported, trusted, able to work in a

---

[24] Think about it. No, still don't get it? Say it out loud.

flexible environment, and left to prioritise for their self when they need to work late, come in early or send an email at 11pm.

An office should be a place to encourage contribution, not to control. As I repeat constantly throughout this book; "the nature of work is evolving and people's expectations of their workplace are changing. Technology is impacting both where and how we work, and issues of interaction, collaboration and business identity are being challenged as we become increasingly free to operate remotely." I didn't say this, those smart people over at unwork.com did.

They go on to say that *boundaries are being blurred*, but increasingly the balance encroaches upon the home life and offices are becoming increasingly a place where individuality is stamped out. Rules are set up to limit internet access, the use of personal mugs and photos of family on your desk, my daughter's company even has a 15 minute rule on coffee and toilet breaks per morning or afternoon (I so need to get into that company!). But the key weakness even in organisations that aren't so restrictive is that they think office redesign begins and stops with technology, when in fact it should begin and end with the people who will use that office.

Or worse, they look at trendy hi tech companies like Facebook or Google and decide to emulate that without really understanding why Google created their community space offices in the first place. So they install a slide in the middle of the office and expect everyone to use it so they express their individuality. An oxymoron if ever there was one.

A better approach is to think about how your people will integrate with office furniture, equipment AND clever use of office space to lower frustration, improve lighting and reduce a sense of oppression within the office environment. For example, a simple evaluation of what your current or refreshed IT equipment needs are before you decide on the office furniture order means you can design *in* the best way to incorporate the features of your IT platform and design *out* the frustrations that employees will feel trying to get comfortable whilst using that IT on a desk or unit that means cables are too short to reach the power supply without it being in a strange angle.[25]

Take a bite...

Think about when you have had to do something you really didn't want to do but felt you had to because you felt it was expected of you. Describe it on paper. Then think about how it made you feel. Then ask yourself, as you start to write an email at 11pm to send to your PA, how will he/she feel when their Blackberry buzzes to say: "You've Got Mail."

The reality is, we will ALL be far more effective when we *want* to do something, rather than just because we're simply paid to do it[26] or because we feel a pressure to do it.

It therefore becomes the great manager's duty to create a working environment where people simply cannot wait to get into the office because they have a great place to work, lots of friends they want to catch up with, and a management team that really respect, support, and look after them. Telling people to stop talking so much does not achieve this. Letting people think they have to work late every night does not achieve this.

Creating an environment where people can have a laugh, enjoy banter with their colleagues, feel relaxed and inspired and even plan a social night out as a team (or go for lunch even, wow, major concept!) will most certainly achieve this. And once one department or team changes

---

[25] A great company who are bring these concepts out to the business community is Dale Office Interiors- see http://www.daleoffice.co.uk/

[26] Of course for some people this IS a great reason to do something, but many start to see themselves as being a *wage slave*. Really makes you want to work hard doesn't it!?!

the rules of the game, you watch how other parts of the company start to change too.

Oh and one final thing. When your team are happy, feeling inspired and being incredibly productive because they *want* to be, you're happy too. *Simples.*

Try something else...

For more thinking on changing the culture of your organisation, or the way you engage with your work force, see Principle 4: The Court Jester Principle.

Coping with indigestion?

Q: What about the slackers? Won't they just spend all day yakking with their colleagues and not do any work?

A: *There are always going to be people who try to take advantage. What you need to be aware of is that these people will be trying really hard not to do work even under your current regime. But there is a world of difference between becoming the manager that supports his or her team and cultivates an environment where everyone feels relaxed and engaged- and a manager who tries to be everyone's best friend. You must not forget discipline within this. Have fun with your team, certainly, but not at the expense of being professional.*

11

Up The Workers!
Not everything is down to bad management!

There are some employees who just want to cause problems. They are set in their ways and do not want to change, or don't understand why an organisation has to employ certain strategies, or simply don't like who they work for.

We all know who our trouble causers are! You might even be one of them. You see it as your duty to give it to the man, to make sure they know they might have your flesh but they don't have your dignity. But this is missing the point: fighting change for the sake of fighting change means YOU lose.

There are some employees who are disruptive on purpose. They resist change, even when they can actually see the benefit in making it. That's why they shout down the hosts of hell when a new selling strategy, or performance management framework, or new IT system or process is implemented. It isn't that they think the change is a bad idea, it's that they have an identity to maintain.

That identity usually is one of these:

1. **They are the keeper of the company ethics and morals.** These are the people who believe they are morally superior to those working around them. They are the equivalent of the Mary Whitehouse brigade: they must see all the corruptive images because, whilst they are immune to corruption, the rest of us with our lax moral fibre and low intelligence are not.
2. **They are the protector of workers' rights.** They see it as their duty to challenge all decisions and changes made by management that, in their opinion, change any of the agreed terms of employment for themselves or others.
3. **They are a rebel.** They must therefore be seen to constantly, well, rebel against authority.

Now, I want to be very clear here. I am not attacking trade unionists, people with religious faith, or true mavericks. I am however most definitely on the case of those pseudo-people who try to hide behind some half-baked identity as an excuse to simply be disruptive so they can be the centre of attention.

For example, I have worked closely with two trade union representatives in the last decade. Let's call them Collette and Joe.

Words of Wisdom

"There is only one boss. The customer. And he can fire everybody in the company from the chairman on down, simply by spending his money somewhere else." - Sam Walton

Collette would fight for her workers whenever it was clear that a massive, unannounced change was coming that would severely affect their agreed terms, or when an individual had been subjected to harassment of some kind. The rest of the time, she was extremely pragmatic, would proactively consult and negotiate with management and employees alike, and would work just as hard to implement change that benefited the organisation (and therefore everyone) as any manager would.

The management enjoyed working with Collette- any ideas bandied about were done in a spirit of looking at the common good. There were no agendas, or suspicions. Schemes became dramatically improved and implemented with a minimum of fuss. The environment was one of cooperative working.

Take a bite...

Analyse your behaviour over the last month at work whenever change has been announced. Did you look at it with suspicion? Did you ignore it? Did you rant constantly at colleagues about how unfair the change was? Did you try to see the positives? Did you go back and make constructive suggestions on how to improve it? If your management team shut you down when you tried to make constructive suggestions, why was that?

Joe on the other hand was old school leftie. Management and authority were to be viewed with suspicion and disdain. They were always out to screw the workers so better to screw them first. He would want massive consultation and ballots on even the most minor change to practice, and if the delays meant the company losing money or competitive edge, then so be it. He had done his job. And if that meant the company might have to lay off half his members next year, that didn't matter because he would call a strike.

This management team didn't work so well with Joe. I started to bypass him in the end and work directly with employees, simply because I knew he would waste precious time and energy that would impact negatively on everyone in the long run. Because of this, a different outlook on schemes was lost. They weren't as user friendly as they could have been, or were even simply presented as a fait accompli. Everyone lost respect for the others point of view and management and work force became us and them.

Of course you don't have to be a trade union rep to behave like Collette or Joe. The question therefore becomes what kind of employee are you?

Are you collegiate? Or are you confrontational?

It's important that you understand the difference and the impact that your behaviour can have on the organisation you work for. The reality is that there are some fantastic management teams and executive boards out there, and some wonderful individual managers also. Not all of them want to screw the workers, many of them want to create a successful venture that benefits everyone, including their employees.

If that is the case but you are coming into constant confrontation with them, then maybe it is your identity and belief system that needs to change. Or maybe it's just something as simple as your approach that needs to change.

Try something else...

For more thinking on changing the way you engage with management, see Principle 11: The Gaia Principle for a better understanding of why you should all be working together for the benefit of everyone else.

In conclusion then, try to change your focus away from the evil that other management teams or individuals have done, and onto how you and your current management team or manager can start to work together for the success of all. After all, I'm spending nearly the rest of this book showing managers and management teams what they have to do to change for the better, so maybe you could give them a chance to do so.

Coping with indigestion?

Q: But later on in the book you say management should embrace their mavericks? I'm confused now.

A: *Mavericks are not purposeless or selfish disruptors. Mavericks are something entirely different and can be a life saver for an organisation. So please do not confuse mavericks with trouble causers, turf protectors, blockers or anti-authoritarians.*

Q: Listen, I am someone who is constructive and diplomatic. Yet my manager always shuts me down. What do you suggest I do?

A: *Is this really the case, or are you just saying it to excuse your behaviour? If it's the former, vote with your feet and get a job elsewhere, unless you know that the manager of the manager has a better outlook and you can engineer some way of getting your suggestions through to him or her where they will be taken on board. Don't do it in a pointed way that tries to get your direct manager into trouble or makes them look bad, just present the facts and let them get on with it. In fact you could even try to make your manager look good, as though they asked you to come up with some new ideas. But then leave your current manager a copy of this book so they know they need to change and encourage you to submit suggestions.*

If none of this possible get another job as soon as possible.

12

Labelling the Point!

Sometimes you just have to SHOUT! And in writing too.

If you've got nothing important to say then say nothing. But if what you have to say is of vital import, then shout it out from the rafters and pin it to every wall in the building.

They say the pen is mightier than the sword, and do you know what, they're right. History is full of civilisations that have toppled because of an idea, because someone carefully crafted an argument on paper or in speech that eventually became the wrecking ball that brought the whole edifice down!

In a time when all around us still seems to be doom and gloom and austerity, and the language of Robert Preston[27] is all about meltdowns, catastrophes and the end of the world as we know it, I thought I would use this chapter to offer a few distinctions to help improve our mood.

---

[27] BBC economics reporter

Words have power, so we should all take care about the choice of words we use to describe our state, or the state of our reality. This was reinforced to me, quite accidentally, in a meeting.

In the usual format we all had to give a few words about who we were, what we did and where we had come from etc. When it got to me, I quipped, "At the age of 45 I've finally worked out what I wanted to be when I grew up." Everyone laughed. I laughed. But later I got to think- people do seem genuinely surprised at my age, and I certainly don't feel my age. According to my daughters, I don't act it either.

But then, what do we mean by "acting our age"? Who defines what our age-behaviour ratio should be? At the age of 50, should I be treating everything seriously, stop playing the X-box, watching scary movies or reading comics?

Well, no.

I have a youthful outlook, and a playfulness that is either infectious or irritating depending on where you are on the age-behaviour ratio. However, it is precisely that youthful outlook that keeps me active, creative, humorous and indefatigable. Listen, launching your own business in the current climate is enough to give anyone the heebeegeebees and I wouldn't do it if I wasn't a natural optimist with a sense of fun. And I do have that sense of fun and playfulness, and part of the reason for that is my use of language when I speak to myself.

What do I mean?

THE PROGRAMMING POWER OF LANGUAGE

Well, in neuro-linguistic programming terms, I am never devastated, though I can be "hacked off". I am not depressed, I am in need of a rest/play. When I'm asked how am I doing, I try not to say, "Fine", I say "Great!" I'm not overwhelmed (anymore), I am simply busy. In fact I would like to change that to "active!" When my partner asks me how am I feeling, I say "in love!" In other words, the choice of words we use on a consistent basis affects how we start to view the reality around us. Our brain, it would appear, is a complex computer that can be programmed to great effect.

Try something else...

For more thinking which can be applied to changing the way you get your message across, see Principle 1: The Caduceus Principle, which explains why careful consideration about what you do and say can mean the difference between failure and success.

Unfortunately, this programming can occur unconsciously too; reactions, habits, responses that are triggered without us even knowing why said reactions occur, are common. Look up Pavlov's Dogs[28] as an example of how we can be programmed like a machine. Words can program us with the consistency of their use- or, and this is going to come as a shock to some of you: in their absence of use also.

George Orwell knew this which is why the insidious evil in 1984 is the use of Newspeak as a control mechanism. In effect, newspeak consistently trimmed down the number of words used in everyday life (or altered their meaning in subtle ways). One can't be a "rebel" if "rebel" as a word doesn't exist in language- and therefore as a concept. If the concept doesn't then exist, what chance then of an action based on the concept being able to occur? If you think this is all psychobabble, you are dead wrong: go ask a cognitive therapist.

But we can use this in a positive way if we seek to strip out the worst of negative descriptions when talking about ourselves or our life. In effect, we remove from our consciousness concepts of devastation, terror and

---

[28] At its most basic level: Pavlov used a bell which he rang whenever his dogs were hungry to the point of salivating. After a while, he could ring the bell and the dogs would start salivating even when not hungry.

overwhelm and replace them with less emotive, more manageable concepts instead[29].

Language is emotive and yet follows the laws of entropy: it descends into the lowest possible state of existence and takes our focus with it. Chaos. Death. Destruction by endless decay. *There's a depression out there and it's all the fault of those lazy benefit scroungers and greedy public sector workers. Not to mention those grasping asylum seekers. Coming over here and stealing our jobs.* Use of language like this is dangerous at best!

Take a bite...

Make a list of every word you use on a consistent basis to describe when you're feeling negative emotions. Then make a list of all the words you use to describe, on a consistent basis, words for when you're in a positive mode. Go on, do it now before you read any further. Two things should be apparent. One, we have a great many more negative emotion words than positive ones. And two, our negative words are much more strongly expressive than our positive ones. So now, take the negative words and look for weaker alternatives. Instead of "enraged" you could choose to say "annoyed" for example.

Now, take all your positive words and strengthen them up. Instead of "Fine" you could say "I'm fantastic thank you!" Trust me, after a while, you will feel your mood generally improve.

---

[29] By the way, this is something our political commentators, politicians, financial wizards and all those other "experts" do on purpose. Castigating vulnerable groups and blaming them for the ills of public finances directs anger way from those in power; creating a climate in which everyone is a potential terrorist or paedophile forces us to live in fear and look to those in power to protect us. All we need to do is give up our liberties. More on this in my book "Conspiracy: Waking Up To The Mind Control in Our Life", coming in 2016.

I can't tell you how mad phrases like those on page 94 make me feel. I do try to moderate my language when re-presenting the Mail brigade chattering to myself, but I do, I admit, tend to fail. However, I digress.

The purpose of this entry is because I want us all to seek to be more positive, more playful and increase our happiness, and that includes in the workplace. To do this we have to change our internal dialogues first before we can change how we view our external realities. One way to do this is to change the balance between the strong negative words and weak positive words and phrases that we use on a consistent basis.

Now, don't get me wrong- I'm not into all that positive thinking stuff. Think and you will make it so is not entirely accurate. You need strategies and distinctions, a great deal of hard work and a lot of additional things too (many of which are discussed in this book, phew!)! These all come with time. But your brain simply cannot distinguish between truth and imaginary. Don't believe me? Okay, go watch a horror film. You know that Freddy or Jason is just a made up character don't you? So why do you squirm so much? Why did you scream out when the alien burst out of John Hurt's chest?

Okay, so I'm keeping this simplistic, but the concept is valid. Go ask any neuro-scientist and they will confirm that, at the deepest level, the brain really isn't able to separate reality and language.

And so, because of this, I just know I am not growing old. I am simply growing.

EMPLOYING WORDS TO MANAGE EFFECTIVELY

I struggled with the above heading because to be honest, one could write a whole book about this subject[30] and in fact, several authors, business leaders and psychology majors have. So I will not rehash old ground or debate points with these writers. Instead I will try to explain

---

[30] In fact, watch out for work by Jodie Houlden of PIQ Development, coming soon.

briefly why taking time and using the right words in a timely fashion when dealing with your employees, executive board members and clients alike is a must and not something to do if you have the time.

Let's imagine you need to implement a new IT system to improve efficiency across the organisation. You also have a huge sales campaign starting in a month that, if successful, will secure the business long term. Both are connected, in that the IT system will improve the speed at which enquiries can be dealt with by the correct team or individual, and process orders that come in.

Do you simply send an email out stating:

"Dear Team

From tomorrow there may be IT service disruption for several days whilst we change over from the OKIKOKI2000 system to the NKOTB3000[31]. This change is essential to improve efficiency across the accountancy, sales and operations departments and needs to be done quickly before the new sales campaign kicks off next month, so that we can cope with the expected enquiries and sales.

Thanks

The Boss"

Well, you could, but there are issues with such an approach, and some simple steps (or thinking exercises) that would mitigate against them.

1. Advance notice is good but 24 hours is not advance notice. Unfortunately there are managers who think they are giving advance notice if they tell you as you leave the office the evening before. They should, of course, be shot. In the meantime what you should do is give as much advance notice as possible and repeat it as many times as possible. This enables everyone to have made plans to cope with delays or errors, or to be aware that such delays may occur on a temporary basis.

---

[31] NewKidOnTheBlock3000. It isn't a real product. I made it up.

2. Furthermore, such an IT change will have potential impact on your suppliers and your clients. They too must be told! You can even turn it into a benefit in that you can invite your client, or supplier account manager, out for lunch or a coffee to go through the changes with them so that you or your account managers can bond with the client.
3. Why are you changing to the NKOTB3000? What are the TRUE benefits to the whole organisation, your suppliers and your clients? These need to be explained briefly. Note, I said benefits and not features. And also note, the benefits will be different for each group, so choose the most relevant ones when you contact them.
4. You may think saying the IT system will improve efficiency is a benefit for the teams involved, but they will feel that what you are really saying is that the departments are inefficient. It may sound like semantics, but words have power, remember? And then to compound this by suggesting that they can't cope in the last sentence is really waving a red flag to the bullocks in the field. No, you must be clear: the new system is there to help staff become even more effective and free up their time as they won't have to deal anymore with the old system's whatever they used to complain about. In effect, you are saying you are doing it to help them in their day to day job.
5. The same clarity must be expressed about the expected future demand to come from the sales campaign. Distinctions and links must be illustrated between the new system and the improved chances of success for the campaign.
6. You must also illustrate why having a successful sales campaign is beneficial for all within the company and how the new system will help in ensuring the campaign's success and long term viability of the company (thereby the pay and conditions of the workforce).
7. Don't just send a blanket email. Have meetings. Put notices up. Have a screen saver countdown. Put it on the intranet, website and social media pages. And do it more than once!

Just a few minutes planning and careful consideration of the words you use will make a smoother transition path for everyone, create less tension and suspicion and foster a greater effort, even subconsciously, amongst your organisation to make the project a success.

Words really do have power. So use them effectively. 'Nuff said.

Words of Wisdom

"Any idea, plan, or purpose may be placed in the mind through repetition of thought." Napoleon Hill

Coping with indigestion?

Q: Surely we've got more important things to be worrying about than the ruffled feathers of a few employees who need to be a bit thicker skinned?

A: *Possibly you have, but why not spare the blushes of the thin skinned so that everything is smooth sailing (if I may be allowed to mix my metaphors)? After all I'm not suggesting you spend weeks planning how to get a message across about some change, event or business need, I'm simply saying, give it some thought before you take it further. After all, it may end up being YOUR blushes that you need to spare.*

Q: Are words really that powerful?

A: *Yes. Tony Robbins uses the following example: say someone says to you that you're mistaken about something. How would that feel? Now, let's imagine they came up and said that you were just plain wrong! Wouldn't that provoke a different emotion within you? Aren't you likely to feel a bit more defensive? Or if they said that they thought you were lying about it, wouldn't that convey a much deeper meaning and challenge to your position and thereby elicit a stronger reaction? It's the same situation, but the choice of words changes the entire dynamic.*

13

Become a Partner, Not a Product!
People can change products easily!

You have the best product on the market. Your services are awesome. So you sell to your customers and everything seems okay. It could be better, but business is okay. Then slowly, your customers decrease and you don't know why.

We all love having customers, but the reality is customers are a fickle bunch. They can change their products because of image, a slightly cheaper price, a more handsome or prettier sales person (er, I've been guilty of that, sorry to be so shallow), or simply for a special offer!

We talked in the last chapter about the power of words, and here is a good example of how words create identities, both for us and for the people we are selling to.

When we view these people as customers that's what they are; customers. Customers have no loyalty to any particular company, product or brand. Don't believe me? Look in your wallet or purse. How many loyalty cards do you have? Or credit cards from different companies? The sad fact is that the vast majority of customers don't feel any emotional bond with the companies they buy from.

Now some forward thinking organisations have thought of that, so they call their customers "clients". "Clients" is a far superior label to put on the people who buy from you. Clients are more personal, it indicates a one to one relationship, and suggests that they are given a special service befitting a higher status within the organisation.

However, client still says someone you sell to. It is still a limiting identity, and clients will still sometimes shop around for a better deal and fall prey to the latest special offer. What you want to be is a partner, and for the people who buy from you to feel that they are partners with you, that you have their best interests at heart, and that any service or product you provide them is to enable them to achieve their goals and objectives.

Notice I said "provide" and not "sell"? You see, when you work with a partner, our descriptive language will change. Your "customer" will come to see your organisation as someone who is an integral part of their business. Now, do you think once a customer starts to see their relationship with you in that light, it might be a lot harder for a competitor who comes along with a "special offer for new customers" to actually steal that "customer" away? You bet it will.

The same principle, by the way, should be extended to *your* suppliers. Get them to start to see you as a long term partner, someone whose continued growth is vitally important to their own- even if that is a long way down the line. Remember, tall trees grow from small acorns.

I'll give you an example of how this process works. There's a small company I've been working with who won a substantial contract working with a council. Let's call the company PP Ltd. The potential for business that could springboard from this contract for PP Ltd is huge, but they had an issue. The staff, whilst enthusiastic, is young and relatively untrained. The owner of PP Ltd, let's call him Joe, had spent the last couple of years growing organically and had determined to recruit and train up local labourers, especially young people who had not been able to find work before.

Now, we should take our hats off to Joe for being ready to do this, but the issue was the opportunity presented by this contract meant that all his staff had to become experts in council legislation, rules and policies. Furthermore, their culture had to change from one of an informal, family-style business, to one that had to present a professional image at *all* times. I'm not saying the staff wasn't professional, but the involvement with the council meant that they had to move to a whole new level.

Words of Wisdom

"I don't want to be just a voice on the phone. I have to get to know these guys face-to-face and develop a sincere relationship. That way, if we run into problems in a deal, it doesn't get adversarial. We trust each other and have the confidence we can work things out." Wayne Huizenga

Furthermore, PP Ltd had to pay out a great deal of money up front to purchase new equipment, IT systems and tracker devices for vehicles and so on. It was a huge commitment.

I was asked to create a programme of change that involved the creation and delivery of training programmes, policy creation covering everything from health & safety and safeguarding to use of mobile devices, and support. Now, normally for such a massive undertaking I would charge around £500 per day (a day being 8 hours), plus expenses.

For PP Ltd, I looked at where they were and where they could be. On the basis of that I charged a flat fee to incorporate all work and expenses. I explained that I was doing this because I want to partner up with PP Ltd so that as they grow, they bring me in to conduct all their training and to provide other services as they evolve.

Joe was really pleased with this, especially as, during the delivery of the policies and programmes, I was flexible enough to adapt to new demands from his client, and also did far more than was initially agreed (extra policies at no extra charge, extra meetings to advise on approach and so on).

It doesn't stop there however. On the back of this, Joe asked me if I knew how he could now start to bid for other local government contracts. I showed him the kind of sites he needed to register with and even prepared some of the information he would need to be accepted as a registrant to get invited to apply for certain tenders.

Take a bite...

Pick an existing customer and look at the profile you have for them. Is the profile very brief? Do you even have a profile? The first thing you need to do is make that profile completely in-depth, as many facts, figures and impressions as possible from as many sources as possible. Once you've done that, analyse what you have and look to see what the potential for that client could be. Write it down. Then align your service or product with that potential future. What extra could you do? What other service/product set or enhancement could you make? Make it into a proposal that focuses on the need of your client, and go to see them personally to go through it with them.

On the back of that, Joe asked me to manage his office and recruit a permanent office manager. Due to various issues and cash flow problems, PP Ltd was experiencing massive growth pains, but because I was not embedded in the day to day operations Joe gets to manage his cash flow and plan or manage his resources much effectively, and concentrate on building his profile and relationship with his major client- and hopefully turn them into a partner, and get them to see PP Ltd as a partner and not a supplier. For me, I get regular income during a tough time economically! Now Joe is launching a new company and who do you think he has asked to help him put that together? Even better, I get a free office as part of the deal, so how much freedom do you think that will give me?

POTENTIAL VS IMMEDIATE

One last thing, in the Take A Bite box on the preceding page, I talk about analysing the potential of your customer and aligning your offering to match that potential. I want to explain a little more what I mean by this.

All too often we look at a customer based on what they spent with us last week or month or quarter and assign resources accordingly. This is because we don't see the potential business we could achieve with that customer. We're only as good as last week's billing, right?

WRONG!

Let me give you an example.

I worked for an IT product and service company many years ago (let's call them PowerIT), a company that quite rightly had decided to move into being a services company where the products became incidental. A new account manager, Brian, had moved from a huge reseller to this company and, having a personal relationship with a senior manager, had set up a meeting at a leading vehicle callout service, a company that would have been a huge win for PowerIT. He wanted to impress the manager with the knowledge and skills at his new company and asked me to come along to do a presentation on technology futures.

The meeting went very well, and Brian handled the objections about the size of PowerIT vs their current IT supplier, which was a huge European reseller based in London, but with offices all over the country and locally to them, where as PowerIT had one office and one warehouse centre some 80 miles away.

However, impressed with us, the manager said he would see what business he could organise for us as a pilot. As you can imagine, Brian was extremely excited by the premise, and on the way back to our HQ called them to say that the client might be placing an order at some point this week and could they make sure it was given priority.

Unfortunately, that wasn't communicated to the teams involved in any order processing. Sure enough, whilst we were still driving back, the client placed an order for 3 PCs, stressing that they were urgent and needed to be with them within 48 hours. The order was submitted to processing, who looked at the order for 3 PCs and then looked at a 40 unit order that was in the process of being picked. The team put the seemingly small order to one side, and, as no-one informed Brian that the order had even come in, it sat there until the 48 hours had lapsed. The client cancelled the order and did not move their account.

Now, am I saying you should ignore existing business? No. True enough, the 40 unit order was from an existing client, but one who bought roughly once a year from PowerIT. They never had any real urgency in their needs and were quite relaxed about when the equipment would arrive.

The issue was that no-one had done a proper profile of the existing company to help the processing staff make judgements on who should get priority. Furthermore, the operations team had been told by the directors that they should always get the volume out first. No-one within the department had any kind of remit to analyse the longer term potential of an order from a new client.

Try something else...

For more thinking on how you should deal with your customers, see Focus Area 16, The Customer's New Clothes.

In conclusion then, and as we have mentioned throughout this book, it's how we focus on our customers that decides on whether they remain customers, or becomes partners in success. The question therefore needs to be: which would you prefer?

Coping with indigestion?

Q: Yeah but that's all well and good if I was running a massive service company but I own a couple of market stalls. How can I build a partnership with people who shop on markets?

A: *The best market traders are those who get to know their customers, by name, and engage in a relationship with them. They start to get a feel for what products the customer is interested in and becomes an expert in that area, offering advice and assistance. They will even direct the customer to other traders who have complimentary products or a specific product the customer wants that they don't provide. Now, as a customer, and you need to go on the market to get your tomatoes, who are you going to go to? The trader who calls you mate or love and takes the money from you, or the one who greets you personally, picks out the best tomatoes and recommends some great complimentary vegetables or cooking tip?*

Q: What if they don't want to be a partner, or try to take advantage of what we're trying to do?

A: *Sadly, as in all walks of life, there will be customers who try to take advantage of what you offer, so then it becomes a judgement.*

There are however 2 simple questions that help you decide whether you decide to hang on in there, or focus your resources on a better potential.

1. Is this due to the culture of my client's organisation, or is it just him? If it is him, is there anyone else within the organisation I could be working with instead?
2. Is the long term potential business I could receive with this client worth the short-term hassle?

If the situation is that the client simply isn't bothered about taking the relationship to the next level, then continue to look after that customer[32], but move your focus onto a client who does.

---

[32] You'll have noticed that I have continued to talk in terms of client and customer in this chapter, and indeed the book. That's because in terms of words using these terms make it easier to differentiate between your company, the people you sell to and the people you buy from. The change in focus comes when you start to apply the principles.

14
Right Person for the Right Job!

Don't use a square tool in a round hole!

It may seem strange that I am advocating you look at your employees as tools, after spending most of the book so far espousing a different way of thinking. In fact, I'm only drawing a temporary analogy, so please read on dear reader.

We have all seen it happen. A great salesperson is made sales manager. A great footballer becomes the manager of his old club. And at best they deliver mediocre results. At worst they are an unmitigated disaster!

To compound on this mistake, I have even seen people promoted into a position of responsibility that actually didn't want to be promoted. They loved what they were doing so much, and they were brilliant at it, that they just didn't want to do anything else. But we make them "move up" anyway, so they can instil whatever they do that is so successful to the wider team or department.

But being fantastic at a job or particular role is a far cry from being an effective people and/or processes manager. Furthermore, the person we have promoted has had no training or coaching in how to be a manager anyway, and starts off by trying to either be everyone's friend, or by being the "I'm-the-manager-you-do-what-I-say!" type of manager who just winds everyone up and loses the respect he or she thinks they will receive.

There is an even worse type of this 'promoting the wrong person for the wrong reason' approach- that of promoting someone to get them out of the way, or as a way to shore up support for the one who has promoted them.

Words of Wisdom

"If the only tool you have is a hammer, you tend to see every problem as a nail." Abraham Maslow

Let me give you an example.

Paul is a man who looks the part. He never has a hair out of place on his head or moustache. He wears only the best, custom made suits and is colour coordinated to a tee. His shoes are unblemished. He has expensive tastes. He also has a smooth tongue that says what people want to hear. He goes into sales and because he impresses the management team so much he is given the biggest account the company has.

Within a year, he had lost it.

But he still says the right things, and offers unflinching support to the MD, so the MD makes him branch manager of the most successful branch. Within 18 months, that branch also closes. But Paul shows quite clearly that it wasn't his fault, it was just bad luck, the economy or bad account management by a couple of account managers that he had subsequently fired. He is then made manager of The New Solutions Team (NST), as the previous manager was not someone who offered unflinching support to the MD and was therefore "let go" when the company restructured and the NST became the New Technologies Group (NTG) so that the former manager couldn't cry constructive dismissal.

Now the remit of the NST/NTG was to identify new technologies and develop a solution or market for it that would increase sales and profitability. As the NST it had been hugely successful because it was staffed with technology experts who had marketing skills. Paul didn't understand technology. In fact he understood it so little that he dismissed the ISDN/fibre optic marketplace as something that would never take off.

Within 9 months, the NTG had lost two thirds of its staff and had lost its competitive edge. But that was because the team were difficult, that they never accepted the change of manager and so on. Paul was subsequently made a Director of the company because the MD needed someone on the board to shore up his authority as other directors were starting to question some of the directions the company had taken.

Eventually however, Paul outlived his usefulness and he was allowed to move onto a company with a glowing reference from the MD. Ironically, the company he became Sales Director of specialised in ISDN and communications technology.

Now, I spent some time describing that situation because I wanted to drive home the point about how we can promote people, or put them into a position, without really looking at what the nature of that person is. Sure, on paper they have the right experience and skills, but what about *them*? Does their temperament make them right for the job? If you're going to make them a manager of a large team, are they someone who has tact and diplomacy, or able to show empathy? Or are they just a type A aggressive?

If you're not considering this in your recruitment or promotion procedures then you're leaving yourself open to some real issues.

Take a bite...

Conduct a skills audit of your staff and a personality test (there are hundreds on the web to choose from). Are BOTH a match for the role that the person fulfils? If not, are there any signs that the mismatch is causing a problem? Remember, some people can adapt their abilities to any role, so you don't necessarily need to think about redeployment. But you still ask these people if they are happy in their role or would they prefer something else instead. Stress that the exercise is to help employees and the company, as well as yourself. Do this process elegantly and with sincerity, do not use it as an excuse to get rid of someone!

I'll give you an example. An airline company was facing a huge number of complaints from customers, and one of their success indicators was the percentage of happy customers. This caused all kinds of headaches. Upon analysis it became clear that the majority of the complaints were coming in from one service area (in fact some 60% if I remember correctly), and around half a dozen employees in particular.

The management team at this airline were pretty smart. They didn't simply fire the employees, they properly analysed the situation. Basically these employees had started off as back office staff, doing a great job managing processes and orders, but had gradually been promoted into roles where they dealt with customers. These people were process-people, not people-people and because of this, their lack of patience or frustration with people would come through.

They moved the staff back into positions where they would be happy, and brought in people who liked working with people to the customer facing roles. They then reviewed other departments and looked at the types of people they had in certain roles. Complaints fell by almost 80%.

However, this management team didn't stop there. They looked to the future and changed their recruitment policy. Applicators for roles that involved dealing with the public were told that they would have to make a short presentation about themselves to the other potential employees as part of the interview process.

What was interesting about this was that the interviewers were not looking at how good a presentation the presenter was giving, they were watching the audience made up of the other interviewees. Those who were attentive, and gave support to the person presenting were automatically through to the next round. Those who were sneering or simply acted as though they were bored were automatically removed from the process.

Over the next year, complaints fell to their lowest level on record.

This is why it is so important to think about the people you are recruiting or promoting.

Try something else...

For more thinking on using the right tool for the right job, see Principle 3: The Jewish Vampire Principle.

There's no doubt that the wrong person doing the wrong job can cause you untold damage in the long run, or even the right person in the wrong job! It is important therefore that we conduct a proper person to role matching exercise. That said, I need to issue a couple of caveats.

Firstly, do not use psychometric tests as the basis for employing someone. They should only be used to give you an indication of the best role the individual would be best placed in. It simply astounds me that companies use these tests to do an initial sort, and some as the basis for hiring a person even when they have done an amazing job. Psychometric tests can be fooled. Also, it really does depend on the mindset of the person being tested on the day. I certainly know I can do the same test 5 times over a period of weeks and you would get 5 very varied sets of results.

Secondly, have more task oriented elements included in your selection process, especially where contact with customers is incredibly important or sensitive. Use tactics like the one employed by the airline company. People think they're being assessed on one aspect, whereas you are assessing the aspect most important to the job role.

Finally, audit your staff constantly and consistently. Don't just blanket reward someone with a promotion if that's not what they want, instead be creative in your rewards system. If someone is doing a fantastic job but doesn't want to move from the job, why change their job just because your policies say so.

It really is that simple.

Coping with indigestion?

Q: What do I do if a skills &personality audit shows a person is completely wrong for the job they are in?

A: *As I said in the Take a Bite section, take a look at the person doing the job and see if there are any causes for concern. Remember, the best personality profile system in the world is still only a guide to a particular period in the life of that person's psyche. If there are problems, analyse what the problems are. Is it the person or the unsuitability of the job? Are they able to do a better job in a different role? Would they like to move to that job if at all possible? (You should also ask a person who appears not to be experiencing problems but whom, on the face of it, is not suitable for the role long term). If there is no role for them elsewhere, or are unable or unwilling to transfer to a different role better suited, then you have to engage your disciplinary process, put the employee on managed measures so that they can either be retrained, or, in the end, let go on capability issues.*

15

Work & Life in Harmony!

Switch off that Blackberry and do something more productive instead!

Ever since the 1950s, we've been promised that technology will deliver a lot more leisure time, the 3 day week or increases in productivity that mean we can retire early. So what happened?

Technology is wonderful. It's also evil. It depends, you see, on how we choose to implement it. The truth is that technology HAS given us the tools to free up more time and make us more productive. Unfortunately, the time it has freed up has been eaten up by greedy capitalists who want a one way information superhighway!

Chances are you are one of those greedy capitalists[33] and you've given all your staff a nice smart-phone so they can be in constant touch with

---

[33] There is nothing inherently wrong with being either a capitalist or greedy from time to time, you just have to learn how to balance that with wider issues.

the office. I mean, it is absolutely vital they answer that email on their way to that client meeting. And if it's important for them to answer that one, then why not the one you send after they get home? And what about the one you need answering when they are on the way to the theatre?

The sad truth is that technology has blurred the lines between work and home life. Unfortunately, in the majority of cases, the blurring is one way. Whilst many organisations think it is okay to call or send txts and emails at 11pm, the same organisations ban personal use of the internet between 9am and 5pm. *Want to pay that really urgent credit card bill, sorry bub, you have to use your lunch hour. By the way, I need your comments on the marketing report. I haven't got it on me at the moment, I'll email it to you tonight.*

Sound familiar?

When I was given my first smart phone, being a technologist I was really thrilled. I mean, calls, txts, internet & emails in one place! Then I noticed it was programmed to come on at 6am and switch off at midnight. I was told that I had to pay for any personal calls but it was okay for the management team to call me at 8pm as I was sitting down to eat with my family.

The first thing I did was reprogram it so I could switch it on and off when I wanted. That didn't fly brilliantly well with the management, until I pointed out that my job description and contract didn't mention anywhere that I had to be at their beck and call outside of working hours and that such a presumption needed to be made explicit in said contracts. Which meant a rewrite of everyone's terms & conditions and a justification to offset UK employment law regulations on hours.

I also pointed out that such a push bordered on harassment and bullying, and in the end it was counterproductive anyway as studies show that people who do not switch off and rest become completely unproductive over time.

And that's the truth that our UK-US macho business culture fails time and again to understand, and there are people reading this right now who still don't understand. Okay, I shall try to explain this concept very simply:

WE HAVE THE LONGEST WORKING HOURS IN THE WESTERN WORLD AND YET SOME OF THE LOWEST PRODUCTIVITY LEVELS.

Now, there are lots of reasons for this of course, but study after study (Work & Pensions, Manpower, EU commission etc- go Google!) show that the more hours a person works the less productive he or she becomes, and eventually a tipping point is reached where any productivity gains made in the short term are wiped out in the longer term slowdown or illness of the employee.

Think about it. It is the story of the woodcutter that I told in Focus Area 4: Have a Plan. The more you work with it, the more you blunt the tool, until jobs take more and more effort to complete. You MUST take time to re-sharpen the tool, or to do maintenance work.

Words of Wisdom

"When people go to work, they shouldn't have to leave their hearts at home." Betty Bender

So as a manager, you should really start to think about these issues whenever you feel the need to send an email to your employees at 10pm as you are leaving the office. There are some very simple questions you can ask first:

- Is it vital to do this now? Or could I send it first thing in the morning?
- Is the extra hour or 2 of output I would get from my staff worth the stress it could cause, or the resentment it might build up?

- If this is important to get done now, what can I give back to my staff because of the lateness of the demand?

If you do work within an environment that regularly needs extra hours or home life hours being sacrificed to the greater good of the company, you MUST take a look at your 9-5 policies. Can your employees do their internet banking or book a holiday online from their terminal without the thought-police smashing down the window and taking them away? If not, change it now and communicate that it has been brought to your attention that the blurring of work-life boundaries has been one way and that you want suggestions about how it can be made more equitable. Do it sincerely and with humility if necessary.

You'll be amazed at how much credit you will create with your staff.

MANAGING MY TIME REALITY

Changing things from on high is all well and good, but changing how time applies to you is important as well.

Let's look at this. Here are some questions for you:

1. Do you check your emails constantly throughout the day?
2. Do you check your tweets, Facebook, txts on a regular basis throughout the day?
3. Do you have an alert set up for when messages come through?
4. Do you leave your work phone on when you're at home?
5. Do you take your work phone on holiday with you? Or to the restaurant or cinema?

If you answered yes to the majority or all of these questions, congratulations, you are completely unproductive.

I know, it sounds counter-intuitive doesn't it? But let's coach this in another way.

You are working on a really urgent report that is also very important. The deadline is tomorrow morning, so you're resigned to staying up late to complete it anyhow. The good news is, you now have a flow, a direction to take it and everything is looking good.

But then, your email alert goes off. So you stop and go look at the email. It's from the departmental head about a meeting later in the week, so you break off what you're doing and send a reply. As you do that, a couple more emails come in and you decide to check them.

Before you know it, 30 minutes have passed before you return to the report. As you start writing however, you notice that you are no longer in flow, and what was the point you were trying to make?

Studies show that if you are interrupted whilst doing a task, it can take up to 20 minutes to get back on task (a recent study indicates it's even more than that but I haven't read it as yet so won't quote it). The bad news for you is that the 20 minutes is constant whether you are interrupted for 30 minutes or 30 seconds.

So you end up feeling stressed and the report is not the best it could be.

I know, I've been there. I was a complete slave to the "what if that email is important" principle. We have been conditioned to react to information flow, whether it's information to us, or a request for information from us. In the end, the constant demands on my so-called rest time (over many, many years) led to a massive meltdown that cost me a great deal in personal losses, and cost the company a great deal of... well, not a lot really. Because the truth is, and I know this is hard to hear, the majority of what you are working on is NOT life or death. The company won't miss the vast majority of things it says it needs if they are not done immediately.

What we all do is confuse urgent things with important things, and because we all like to think we're important people, then we delude ourselves into believing that all the work we do is important too. We must move away from that kind of thinking.

More Words of Wisdom

"One of the symptoms of an approaching nervous breakdown is the belief that one's work is terribly important." Bertrand Russell

Some Simple Concepts and Steps

In the various time management courses I do[34] I give detailed step by step strategies that you can follow: even the Introduction to Time Management Basics (my 2 hour course) has The Six Cycles of Time within it. To write them up would take a book on its own (let me know if you think that's a good idea!), but I will list here some simple ideas for you to apply, and some practical steps for you to take. Do them and you will reduce your stress and become far more productive (even though I hate that term!).

1. **KNOW that 80% of what you achieve comes from 20% of your actions.** If you don't believe me, do a proper analysis of everything you did last week. Add up the hours spent on everything and then deduct the hours that actually achieved good outputs. Divide the second total with the first and multiply by 100. That is the percentage that the second number is over the total number.

    In other words, by identifying and focussing on the actions that will give you the most (relevant) results, you automatically become more productive and less stressed.

2. **Remind yourself that time is an illusion, lunchtime doubly so**[35]. At a quantum level, scientifically speaking, time doesn't exist

---

[34] I have a 2-3 hour Time Basics, a full day workshop and a 3 day workshop that incorporates goal setting and business planning.

[35] The brilliant Douglas Adams and The Hitch Hikers Guide to the Galaxy.

with the same linear predictability that we see at the macrocosm level. Even at our level, time is relative and not at all what we perceive it to be.[36] So don't get hung up on how much time you have!

3. **Take Time to Plan Your Time.** Henry Ford said "Thinking is the hardest work there is, which is probably why so few people engage in it." By taking a time out and scheduling fixed items (meetings etc) and then focusing on what you want to achieve that week, you will be able to save time in the long run, especially as you will be able to link "like" actions together and do them at once.

4. **The Top 6 Pick and Mix.** A very simple strategy to start you getting to grips with time, especially if you think the first three ideas might be a bit too much to just do. Start off every morning by listing everything you need to do and then pick the 6 most important, and do them first in order of importance. Do it every day. Do not be tempted to pick items that are easy to do but not the most important. For example, have you ever noticed that when we've got that really tough piece of work to do, that suddenly we simply must tidy up our desk? Yes, I'm watching you!

5. **Cut it out.** This one is several minor steps that will free up so much time in the day you'll wonder how you ever coped before. However, you must also change your belief systems before, during and after each of these. If you've spent years living in the Reaction Zone, teleporting to the Proactive Realm can be a bit of a culture shock. So keep reminding yourself to relax, and that

---

[36] For a full explanation of time and what it is see my new book "The 50 Year Horizon: Science & Technology for the Non-Believer", out for Christmas (all being well), or come see one of my "Time is Nature's Way of Stopping Everything Happening at Once: Discuss." lectures.

its all for the greater good. Be smug living in your new environment. Okay, the steps are:

a. Turn off all your alerts.
b. Check your emails only 3 times a day: first thing, lunch time and before you leave.
c. Turn off your work phone when you get home, or at the very least for meals, evenings out or watching that programme your partner loves.
d. Don't take your work phone on holidays with you. Ever.

Take a bite...

Imagine you had 30 minutes where you could do anything you wanted to do. What would it be? Write down all the things you could do. For example, in 30 minutes you could:

- Answer 15 or so emails.
- Make 3 phone calls.
- Plan 5 blog posts.
- Get up and go for a brisk walk.
- Watch Friends (again).
- Eat a cheeseburger.
- Update your playlists.
- Play Farmville (I just don't GET the fascination with this).
- Read a chapter in a book (my suggestion)
- Read a related white paper (again, my suggestion)

And how DO we get that extra 30 minutes in the first place???

The easiest way is to switch off the blackberry and do something more productive instead. Yes, I know it's hard, but just try.

So how many steps do you think you can take? Not sure? Okay well, why don't you just pick one for now and give it a go for a while. See how it flies, and then add a second. Gradually you will notice a difference in your stress levels, energy levels and in the time you are spending on family and fun activities. You won't see a decrease in the amount of work you do, and over time, will actually see an increase in what you can achieve.

In effect, stop telling the lie that you have no time. Tell yourself instead that time is about perception, and put your focus on what is truly important to get you out of that immediate stress. Once done, start planning your future focus and stay ahead of the game.

Try something else...

Once you start to focus on what's important to achieve it becomes easier to create your living, breathing plan. See Focus Area 4: Have a Plan.

Coping with indigestion?

Q: Are you saying that if I do all these steps I'll never be stressed again?

A: ABSOLUTELY- not! Stress is a part of life, and I get stressed even now- especially when I think I'm having my time wasted (badly thought out processes, especially e-processes, really send me through the stratosphere). I also sometime take on too much all at once (for example, starting a business, doing a Cert Ed and agreeing to write 2 books). It happens. You and I will never be perfect. You will be stressed. But you won't be as stressed as often or for as long. And the more you use the tools the better your work life balance will become. Or you could book the full time & prioritisation course I do and really grab hold of your life[37]!

---

[37] Sorry, couldn't resist.

Q: But what if one of those emails you've ignored is directly relevant to the report you're writing (or activity you are doing)?

A: *It could well be, but be honest, how many times does something come in right when you are working on it? And even if it does, you're still checking your emails first thing in the morning, after lunchtime and around an hour before you go home. Would a slim chance of losing a little time because you have to make some corrections outweigh the time you've saved by getting the job done? Even if the report is suddenly not needed, you have the material prepared for use at a later date! Don't fall into the trap of believing every item that comes marked for your attention is important.*

16

The Customer's New Clothes!
The customer is NOT always right!

We're all familiar with the clichés. The customer is king. The customer is our boss. The customer is always right. Except, of course, when he's not.

There is no denying that the customer IS your most important asset. You should do everything you can to make the customer feel important, valued, respected. However, you should also have the courage to tell the customer when they are wrong, and even give them the boot as well!

The above line will go against most of the programming you have received throughout your career. Surely the customer is of paramount importance. After all, doesn't it cost three times as much to find new customers as it does to keep the ones you have? True enough, but can you think of any better way to value your customer than by saying he/she's wrong about the solution they want, and recommending one that better suits their needs?

You see, we should always listen to what the customer is saying, even when they don't really mean what they think they mean. In other words, we should listen at all times with the customer's best interests in mind.

Let me give you an example. Years ago I was paid by Microsoft to promote, via a reseller, Microsoft technologies and products, and employed by the reseller to use Microsoft as leverage to reposition it away from being seen purely as a hardware vendor, towards being a services company.

The company, let's call them ITP, had spent a fortune on recruiting and training up some excellent technical staff, and put its sales people through a tough training regime, all to the good. One of the sales people got us a technical appointment with the IT director of a big financial services company in London. They had an antiquated network, based on old Novell Netware technologies, and a basic email system. He had heard about the growing power of integrated network technologies that were marketed as 'Groupware'. He had already received a pitch from Microsoft who was obviously keen to establish the new Exchange server technology in the City. If we won the deal, it would be ITP's first true services contract.

Words of Wisdom

"Always think of your customers as suppliers first. Work closely with them, so they can supply you with the information you need to supply them with the right products and services." Susan Marthaller

We listened to the client tell us what he wanted to do, but our head of services wanted a little more detail about the current needs and limitations. He asked some seemingly innocent questions that actually got the client to think more about the specific issue he needed a solution for. The issue, as he saw it, was that their email was not integrated to other systems, and that there was no online collaboration tool, something he saw as being increasingly important as the company expanded its overseas offices. He also thought the world wide web (as most people called it then) was something they should be looking at.

I then weighed in with this question: What was most important to the company? Increased email capability, or collaboration tools and integration with the web? Without hesitation, he said collaboration and web.

I therefore recommended that he switch over his network to Windows NT, with workstations upgraded to NT workstation. I then added however that he should seriously look at Lotus Notes for his groupware and web integration services. Lotus, recently purchased by IBM, had by far the most advanced and properly integrated groupware technology. Furthermore, I knew that Lotus would integrate better into the IBM mainframe systems that ran the information and database services the client relied upon. IBM and Microsoft were bitter enemies at the time.

The client's reaction was: "Sorry, what did you say?"

I repeated that he should move all his servers and desktops to the NT platform, and use Lotus Notes for the groupware, web and email services.

Again, he begged my pardon. "What about MS Exchange?" he then asked.

Exchange is an excellent email platform with good groupware capability, I replied, but Notes is an excellent groupware platform with good email capability. It all comes down to what you think is more important.

My services manager agreed with me that Notes would be a better solution in this case.

Again the client was confused: "But you're the Microsoft Product guy!!"

"I know," I said, "and Microsoft will get business from this deal. But I've listened to what you have said, and I think Notes will future proof you more than Exchange. Besides," I added, "I would rather give you a solution that you really need than an easy sell because that way we can become long term partners." We offered to set up proof of concept labs showing Exchange and Notes to help him make a decision.

Later that month, we heard we had won the deal. The IT director even rang our Sales Director and told him we had won not because we were the cheapest (because we weren't), or the one with the best record (which we clearly weren't, this would be our first services contract), but because he felt we had really listened to what was needed and were the only company that had offered a non-100% Microsoft solution.

Sometimes, it seems, the customer is quite happy to be directed. And that, dear readers, is what you must learn to do.

You see, I knew the client had only heard of Exchange and I could have done what our competitors had done and recommended the easy sale (made even easier by the fact Microsoft were offering a higher soft dollar[38] at the time). Instead we truly listened to what the customer needed and not what he thought he wanted. It is a fine line you have to tread, but in the end the customer will respect you more if you tell them that they are in fact naked and not wearing a golden cloak.

PUTTING THE CUSTOMER FIRST

There are times of course that you must put the customer first and it always amazes me that the same organisations that preach the customer is king don't actually have policies in place that support the public statements.

One company I worked for, a huge multi-national IT manufacturer and services organisation, had dedicated customer parking in its car park like

---

[38] Soft dollar was rebate on spend in the form of money to the marketing budget.

most companies do. The car park however was behind the building, with reception at the front. It could take as much as 5 minutes to walk from the rear car park to the reception area. There were around 10 car spaces right outside the reception area of course, but these were reserved for the company directors. Customer does NOT come first then, especially if it rains.

The IT arm of another large multinational technologies company went a stage further. In a meeting in France, the Senior VP of European Operations announced that effective from the following month, all their desktops and laptops would be shipping with Windows Me. I put my hand up and said, you mean all the consumer models, right? No, he snapped back, ALL models.

So I asked, "But there will still be a dual boot option where the client can choose what the installation will be out of the box?"

NO he snapped back a little louder. "All models will ship preconfigured with Me."

For those of who remember Me it was the version of Windows that made Vista positively the most reliable OS ever. In comparison with Me of course. The product was a disaster.

Try something else...

For more on how you relate to the customer see Focus Area 13: Be a partner not a product.

Now, I had just come from 5 years of selling IBM and Microsoft solutions to corporate UK and knew that even Microsoft were telling businesses in the UK *NOT* to upgrade to Me. It was aimed purely at consumers and was not robust enough for business reliance. I pointed this out to the VP, who became so angry that *my* boss started kicking me under the table. I ignored him and carried on, warning everyone around the table that, in the UK at least, shipping every model with Me would kill the IT company stone cold dead within 6 months. The product was simply not suitable for business users, and we would be doing them a disservice by trying to pretend it was.

To which the VP snapped- "I am a President of this Company and you will do as I say!! Your customers will have to get used to a new platform!"

Of course they didn't and sales of the company's computers crashed almost as fast as the OS did. Although I was wrong, the company didn't go out of business in 6 months. It took 9 months before the computer arm was shut down.

Take a bite...

Analyse all your processes. Are they designed to make systems easier (or cheaper) for your organisation, or for your customer? Any that do not have the customer in mind should be scrapped and replaced as soon as possible. Patricia Seybold[39] identifies 5 basic premises you should start with on behalf of your customer:
- Don't waste our time!
- Remember who we are!
- Make it easy for us to order and procure service!
- Make sure your service delights us!
- Customise your products and service for me!

The point I am trying to make here is that all decisions MUST involve the needs of the customer right from the start, not as a bolt on later.

---

[39] In her brilliant books "Customers.com" & "The Customer Revolution". For an excellent roadmap on how to develop systems, principles and services focused around the customer, I cannot do any better than to direct you to these books.

But understand also that sometimes you have to work to meet the need of the customer and not the want, and if that means you sometimes gently ease the customer down a different road, you must work out the best way of doing that and then implement it as soon as possible. Burying your head in the sand and taking the money and running (to mix my metaphors again) is not an option.

Remember also that each customer is unique and the method of approach for one may not necessarily work on another. One aspect that is the same however, is that no matter how much the customer protests their need, you are acting in the best interest of that customer- and that will eventually win through.

Coping with indigestion?

Q: I'm confused. One moment you're saying the customer isn't always right and the next you're saying we have to put them first in everything we do. Which is it?

A: *Why is one contradicting the other? By putting the customer first in everything you do aren't you automatically going to want to make sure that the choices he/she makes are the right ones for the customer? Remember, the point of what I am saying here is that whilst the customers' needs are paramount, their wants may be directly opposing those needs. If nothing else, an outsider can sometimes see what's wrong inside a system better than those who are inside the system.*

Q: What if the customer simply doesn't want or believe us about the right product?

A: *This is when you must be prepared to walk away from a deal. I know that sounds painful but here's the truth. The same customer who won't listen to you when you try to recommend a better solution will be the same one that blames you when the one you have supplied/installed on HIS insistence goes wrong. It won't be his or her selection that is the problem; it will be your faulty implementation or installation, or your lack of proper support. It could cost you a great deal of time and resources to put it right and do nothing to limit the PR damage that could occur. It's where that huge NHS IT project went wrong: the supplier listened to what the customer said they wanted, and didn't do due diligence on what was actually needed, or indeed possible. Who got the most blame? That's right, the IT services company which was accused of being over-priced, inept and poorly project managed.*

17
Stimulation Through Diversity!
Dare to think differently and stand out from the crowd!

Every organisation these days has to have equal opportunities and diversity policies (or at least a single equal opportunities and diversity policy), but having a policy and understanding the wider impact a celebration of diversity can bring you are two entirely different things.

Diversity isn't just about recognising the different cultural needs of different ethnic minorities, as some Diversity policies would have us believe with their narrow focus. Diversity extends to everyone and every aspect of life, and recognising diversity is nowhere near as powerful as utilising the skills and backgrounds of what comes out of both a diverse workforce and marketplace!

Hands up if you have done your equal opportunities and diversity training! Keep your hands up if you've ever thought about diversity in any terms outside of that training. Keep your hands up if you are aware that recognising diversity does not simply mean that you're not a racist.

Not many left are there.

There's nothing wrong with the implementation of diversity policies throughout the private and public sectors, in fact on the face of it such a growing awareness about cultural differences and the overt and covert (and sometimes unintentional) exclusion of ethnic minorities from positions within an organisation or wider society is all to the good.

The issue is how the implementation has been, well, implemented. The narrow focus of diversity policies mean that a wider understanding of the power to be found in diversity is not recognised because whenever we think about differences we tend to focus on ethnic or cultural (or religious) differences and about the policies that keep us on the right side of the law.

By doing so we miss out on so much more.

THE THREE LAWS OF DIVERSITY.

For the purposed of this book, I want to first expand our awareness of what diversity is and where you will find it. I then want to give you three simple laws to uphold that will enable you to maximise the potential to be found in *truly* recognising diversity for what it is.

The first place you will find statements about diversity is, of course, where the legal definition of what diversity is fits into the laws, regulations and practices of your company. In the UK, diversity can be described as celebrating differences and valuing everyone. Each person is an individual with visible and non-visible differences and by respecting this everyone can feel valued for their contributions.

This implies a number of conditions and characteristics. Diversity, on the most basic level, therefore encompasses visible and non-visible individual differences. It can be expressed in terms of gender, ethnic minorities, the disabled and so on, and where those people are in terms of management positions, job opportunities, terms and conditions in the workplace etc.

This of course is where the majority of us focus our diversity thinking.

But we should look wider. In terms of businesses and their workforces it should also be about valuing and reaping the benefits of a varied workforce that makes the best of people's talents whatever their backgrounds. I have no doubt that your policy mentions this somewhere within it, but does your organisation truly embrace what this statement means?

Words of Wisdom

"I am a possibilist. I believe that humanity is master of its own fate... Before we can change direction, we have to question many of the assumptions underlying our current philosophy. Assumptions like bigger is better; you can't stop progress; no speed is too fast; globalization is good. Then we have to replace them with some different assumptions: small is beautiful; roots and traditions are worth preserving; variety is the spice of life; the only work worth doing is meaningful work; biodiversity is the necessary pre-condition for human survival." Robert Bateman

The Skills for Business agency say this: "Embracing equality and diversity brings to an organisation a wide range of experience, ideas and creativity whilst giving the individual employee a feeling of being enabled to work to their full potential."

This should be more than just words and a tacit agreement that you will support a diverse workforce. You must actively implement systems and processes that allow that diversity to truly express all the ideas, beliefs, information and experiences that can be utilised by your organisation to grow and/or be more effective.

By emphasising the positive benefits of diversity, such as proactively drawing on a wider pool of talent and rewarding the contributions accordingly, you also positively motivate those employees and meet the needs of a wider customer base. After all, a positive and happy workforce is a positive and effective selling machine!

The other diverse area you should look at is the area of belief and opinion within your workforce, supplier and customer bases. This does not equate to diversity of cultural beliefs. I am talking about the differences of opinion within each and every individual. The old adage that one's meat is another's poison is what I am trying to get at. You might make changes to the way a system is developed and one customer and member of your staff will be really pleased with the changes. But will all? Is there going to be some client or employee that feels the changes have affected them negatively? If so you need to find out why and assess the likely impact so you can either improve the system further, or put in place a mitigation strategy to reduce the potential impact on other clients or employees that may have similar concerns.

Thirdly, there is the diversity of your market. How do you segment your market? Is it as tightly defined as you have thought it to be? Can you identify a possible niche, connected to your primary marketplace, and extend your current products and services to reach that niche? Your marketplace will diversify into new areas of focus, interest and even demographics at an ever increasing rate. If you're not constantly looking at what fads and trends your marketplace exhibits you could suddenly find yourself out of the game completely.

Lastly, there is the diversity of your own belief system and what relation it bears to the reality at the coalface. The quote in the words of wisdom section by Robert Bateman states this far more eloquently than I could. You must constantly challenge your assumptions and beliefs for your organisation to continue to prosper. At your most basic thinking, you must remind yourself that the: "...significant problems we face cannot be solved at the same level of thinking we were at when we created them." Albert Einstein said that. Smart man.

Try something else...

Principle 5: The Round Table Principle covers many aspects that relate to the need to constantly change and update our thinking, as well as looking at the systems and processes you should consider putting in place.

So, given we've talked about diversity being so much more than a policy to admire and follow, what are the three laws I mentioned? Good question, I am so pleased you asked.

Without further ado, here they are:

Law 1. For every diverse opinion you fail to take account of, you severely damage the long term security of your business. In other words, by failing to act when a complaint or suggestion for improvement comes in, you risk allowing your company to stagnate from lack of innovation, or become known as the bad boy of business through bad mouthing. Remember, there is an old saying that change comes through adversity. Wouldn't it be much smarter to make the change before adversity comes knocking at your door?

Law 2. No market remains the same; it will diversify into new zones. As we discussed, you might be the biggest and best widget maker and own 90% of the widget market. And you may have been that way for the last 20 years. But are you monitoring trends in the wider marketplace? That is, what are the trends in the marketplaces of the companies who buy your widgets? Look at the Post Office (or Royal Mail as our foreign cousins most likely recognise as a label). It completely dominated the letter marketplace for decades, even after competition regulation was relaxed. But it ignored the internet and the growth of email until it was far too late. Now, Royal Mail struggles to survive.

Law 3. Everyone connected to your organisation has some idea, experience, contact or skill that can be exploited by your organisation to increase your success and viability. I hate the word 'exploited' but it serves its purpose here. What I mean is "stuff" that you can utilise effectively to give you some competitive edge. This whole idea is discussed in depth in Principle 5: The Round Table Principle so I won't labour the point too much here. Suffice to say: ignore the wealth of useful "stuff" that your staff, clients and suppliers hold on to and you are really missing an opportunity. Or indeed, many opportunities.

Take a bite...

Take a look at your equal opportunities and diversity policy or policies. Do they say anywhere within them that you will PROACTIVELY recognise the wealth of experiences, skills and cultural knowledge that all your employees possess? If it doesn't, change the policy and conduct a whole new focus programme that embeds this new policy within the workplace, and provides an arena for new thinking to be input.[40]

So there you have it, 3 simple laws to programme into your brain whenever you are reviewing your business, or making changes to

---

[40] Yes, I know I just spent most of this chapter stressing that we needed to move away from the simple definition of diversity as being part of a workplace policy to combat racism, but you have to start somewhere, and let's face it, if you don't even have a proactive enlargement of focus here, you're not going to make much progress on the other diversity concepts are you?

processes, products or systems. Ask the right questions and you'll be fine.

Coping with indigestion?

Q: Are you saying that we've got our diversity policy wrong when we focus on recognising our cultural, ethnic or ability differences?

A: *No, but I am saying such a narrow definition by default causes too narrow a focus on how a recognition and celebration of diversity can truly benefit your organisation. You need to diversify your view of diversity.*

Q: Okay, okay I get the drift. But what tools can I use to really embed diversity of thinking within my organisation and reap the rewards?

A: *There are several strategies and physical tools that you can use, and these are discussed in The Round Table Principle later on in this book.*

You can also take part in The Thinking Environment movement, as created and discussed by Nancy Kline in her books 'Time to Think' and 'More Time to Think.' Now, be warned, Nancy is a bit tree-huggy-hippy in her prose and even I was put off by her writing style (as I'm sure some of you are by mine), however please stick with it because the thinking behind The Thinking Environment is actually spot on and the process itself is clearly laid out and hugely effective.

18
Flex That Decision Making Muscle!

Take charge or someone else will do it for you. And they might not have your best interests at heart!

We all joke about making executive decisions, but the reality is that we've created a climate of fear that most definitely dissuades us from making key decisions just in case we make the wrong one. In effect we've got into a state of learned helplessness.

Making decisions is tough enough without being afraid that if you get it wrong the whole world will come crashing down. So we stagnate. Our business stagnates. Our home life stagnates! But the fear of punishment is greater than the uncomfortable feeling caused by stagnation. So we do nothing until it's probably too late.

It is a sad state of affairs when we are actively discouraged from taking charge, making decisions and moving things forward. It never ceases to amaze me when people seem incapable of making even the most simplest of decisions- even down to where do you want to go for lunch!?!

Why is this? When did we become such a bunch of weak-willed androids unable to do anything unless we're directed to do it?[41]

Sadly, the history of it is embedded within generations of misguided control and protectionalism that has created a culture of fear, suspicion and downright hostility toward anyone who steps up and makes decisions without authority from the person directly above. And the world's economy is struggling because of it. Even worse, our ineffectiveness in making our own decisions or challenging the direction from above when it makes no sense has spread into all aspects of our life. Our communities are degenerating around us generation by generation, people are meaner and more selfish, and generally more miserable. And all because we don't know how to make decisions on a regular basis that will move us in a positive direction.

It starts at our schools when bright but challenging young people are shut down and told to shut up by often over-worked and stressed teachers and continues into our work life by managers who simply don't know how to manage.

Words of Wisdom

"The greatest mistake you can make in life is to be continually fearing you will make one." Elbert Hubbard

Let me give you some examples of where I have seen such cultures of stagnation created. I went to work for a large corporation some years

---

[41] There's a very sinister reason too- my third book "Conspiracy: Waking up To The Mind Control in Your Life" will explain all this. Should be in 2016.

ago to develop some worldwide strategic partnerships. They sold media based technologies to TV and other media companies around the world, but also bespoke systems for government agencies. One target client was the Ministry of Defence who were looking to integrate various information feeds into a digitally managed environment, which they could also search.

Now, before I took on the job with this corporation, I was asked to do a keynote end of conference speech on the future[42] by Fujitsu-Siemens to their top clients. In the audience was a senior IT chap from the MOD, and he asked me if I would come and do the same pitch to his management team. I explained that I was now working for this corporation so it would be as their representative and in the form of an ITu[43], to which he had no problem at all.

Take a bite...

Make a list of 3 things that you've been putting off doing. Write them down. Then write down a reason for each why you must decide to do these three things. Finally, decide to do one action against each to complete these three items and do these actions today. Write down how you feel once you have completed them.

At this stage, I did not know that the MOD was a target client, and a week later I was firming up the details with the contact when someone started going wild behind me. He was the account manager tasked with

---

[42] A variation of my "The 50 Year Horizon: Science & Technology for the Non-Believer" lecture (and soon to be published book of the same name)

[43] The IT Update was a programme I created that presented to clients technological futures that may impact on their business (positively or negatively). I did NOT promote any company I was working for during the sessions, but afterwards we would go for lunch or dinner, and the account manager would then be able to chat to the clients. Not a single ITu I delivered failed to generate income.

breaking into the MOD and he had been trying for a couple of years to do so. He was understandably curious as to why I was talking to the MOD. You can imagine how excited he was when I told him about the talk and the ITu programme that I was going to deliver, and I was thrilled because here would be an early win for me at my new company.

So we planned the session together, me making clear what the rules of engagement were, he suggesting some of the technological areas I should look at that the MOD would find really interesting. We were set to go.

But then a few days before the session we were dragged into an office and told that we couldn't do it. I was astonished. I went beyond astonishment when I was given the reason for it. Only *directors* are allowed to make presentations. Now, understand this: I had been developing and delivering presentations for some 10 years by this stage of my career. I had a track record of unparalleled success in generating sales from effectively not selling but instead delivering information and strategies that the client could put to use immediately. We tried to argue the case but we were effectively shut down and told to cancel the appointment and reschedule so that a director could find the time to go.

The MOD had already made a lot of effort to get the senior people together for that date, and given the short notice we gave them for cancelling, they were not happy. The meeting never happened, and my company never got into the MOD.

My astonishment doesn't end there. A few weeks later, I got a chance to see these directors in action at the annual internal conference. They were terrible, sounding like a robot reading their scripts without any intonation or emotion. They even read so-called jokes word for word at the same pace, and I swear you could almost see the moment where the lectern must have said: PAUSE FOR LAUGHTER. No-one laughed, except in embarrassment at the realisation that they were supposed to have laughed.

Now, think about this: how motivated do you think that account manager was going to be in future about trying creative ways of opening doors to new accounts? How motivated do you think I was about bringing old contacts from my corporate days into this organisation?

That's right: not very.

Another example is from when I was just starting out as a consultant. A social enterprise had been set up to deliver an environmentally friendly service whilst providing a platform for people with disabilities or who were returning to a work environment after many years off through illness. The only problem was that the town where they were running the service couldn't care less about health or the environment. It was going to take a lot of effort and expenditure to first change the culture of the town before the service would break even. I was asked to step in and care-take the organisation which had been haemorrhaging cash for several months.

I therefore added a couple of other services, related but different. For example, I approached schools and arranged to take all their old PC equipment for free, rather than for them to pay to have it removed, along with a guarantee that any data would be irreversibly deleted. The reaction was incredible and pretty soon we had 100s of systems. I then did a PR campaign to the local papers about our offer of cheap PCs for individuals and community groups. We also did local computer marts.

Sales were excellent and we made enough money to cover the running costs of the business, even though we were heavily subsidising the main service. I even hired another employee who was an IT expert, but whom had not worked due to mental illness for a couple of years. After a few weeks I was asked to come to a meeting with the Chair of the managing committee, so off I went, thinking that I was about to be praised for being so creative.

Instead I was lambasted for over-stepping my remit. Particular emphasis was placed on the successful PR reporting we had received about the PC recycling initiative, and my hiring of the employee. I couldn't believe it. Furthermore, other initiatives that I had put in place to earn income from multiple streams whilst we were spending a lot of money on developing a shop front for the "core" business were reversed. I was told I had been "hired to manage the day to day business, not to run it!" and that I had to focus only on expanding the core business (that is, their baby).

In the end I had no option but to leave as I knew the core business would kill the company as it simply could not generate anywhere near the income required in the short to medium term. I left, strongly recommending that they withdraw from their existing business model and move into other service areas instead. They didn't do it. Within six months, the company was bust and the 12 or so staff who, having being reintroduced back into the work environment, were once more "on the scrapheap".

Now, don't get me wrong. I am not presenting all this to say I am brilliant and everyone else is wrong. The people who set up this latter venture were passionate about their reasons for setting it up in the first place, really wanted to help people get back into a work mentality in a fully supportive way, and truly wanted to help the environment. But they were blinded to the simple fact that their business model simply would not work where they were based.

Try something else...

To help you become more confident in your knowledge or skills, and thereby more able to make a decision, see Focus Area 2: become your own expert.

For myself, even whilst I have been writing this book, I have made some real humdinger mistakes. I made a tactical error in taking on a 3 month contract that I mistakenly thought would still allow me to continue building my business. Instead it was the hardest work I have ever done- trying to teach a couple of hundred 16-19 years olds who no one else wanted to teach. By the end of the third week, I had nothing left over to come in and then work on the rest of my business. My part time assistant was also drawn away at the same time on her placement that was part of her course. By the time the contract had finished, it was Christmas. In effect, I felt that I had to start the company all over again!

The difference between me and a great many others however, is that just because I made a wrong decision, it does not mean that I will be afraid of making a decision tomorrow.

So what makes me so different? Why am I unafraid to make decisions, even when sometimes I make the wrong decision?

The answer to that is because of my belief sets. I live (or at least try to) by several very simple principles that are installed as firm beliefs. They are not things I think I should do, or things I might do when I consciously remember to do them. They are embedded deep within my psyche. It all ties in with what we discussed in Focus Area 1, on suspending your disbelief. Your beliefs control your destiny.

So what are these beliefs then?

BELIEFS THAT MAKE DECISION MAKING EASY

These core beliefs are as follows:

1. **I would rather make 10 decisions and get 2 or 3 wrong than make no decisions at all.** This is also the first thing I tell anyone who comes to work for me: make your decisions, don't worry if you make the wrong one because so long as you realise you've made a mistake and deal with it, you'll have also made 2, 3 or 4 decisions that were the right one and moved my business (or my objectives) on accordingly.

I am not saying that you as boss should absolve yourself of all responsibility. I am saying that you should show your team that you trust their abilities. You should have regular reviews with your team especially if you know you've handed a massively important piece of work to them. But do not stand over their shoulders or make it so that they have to check every little thing with you. In that case, you might as well do it yourself because you are causing delay at every level of the piece of work.

So change your belief here. If you have 3 people working for you and in a week they make 10 decisions each. Even if they get 3 decisions each completely wrong, you'll still have moved everything on at a ratio of 21:9. And even the things that go wrong can be valuable so long as you have created an environment where the team feel they can come to you and put their hands up, knowing you will support them in sorting it out, rather than reprimanding them for making a mistake.

2. **I never fail, I only learn something new.** I discussed this earlier in the book. So, if you look at the last paragraph above, as soon as your team member comes to you with a "hey boss, I think I might have screwed up" you get them to analyse the situation for you, you both work on a solution, and then you both review what happened and how such an occurrence can be avoided in the future. This might be a new process or making an existing process more robust. It might be the only lesson to learn is: *we won't ever do that again.*

Both 1 and 2 of course apply to how you would behave in your own thinking processes when YOU screw up.

3. **We will all make mistakes because no-one is perfect.** Perfection ladies and gentlemen, does not exist. Therefore pushing yourself to be perfect makes no sense. Bullying your

staff because you expect them to be perfect makes even less sense!

Instead, strive to make yourself and your team outstanding. Outstanding brings a buzz and energy all of its own, and it means that people can push themselves and will want to push themselves to become outstanding. Deep down we know we can never be perfect, so we don't wholeheartedly follow through.

So if we know we can't be perfect and that no one else is perfect, then why should we be afraid of making a mistake? We shouldn't.

4. **The more we make decisions the easier it becomes.** You see what we often forget is that our brain is like the rest of our body, if we don't use it then it becomes weak and flabby. Now I know you're thinking I'm getting confused between organs and muscles, but am I really? If you don't exercise your heart, doesn't it get clogged and weak and flabby at pushing that blood around your body? It's the same with the brain, and decision making requires you to flex your decision making muscle. The more you flex it the stronger it becomes. The less you use it, the weaker it becomes. And I could go one step further and start talking about habit forming. Wouldn't it be great if you could make decision making a habit?

There is also a danger in allowing others to make decisions that directly affect you. The people above or around you may not necessarily have your best interests at heart, or they may have but make a decision for the wrong reason or in the wrong state of mind. For example, if you are unable to make a decision about something, often someone will make your decision for you in a state of frustration. Now, in that state, how effective would that decision really be?

No, the only way to really be outstanding is make your own decisions. If you work in an environment where decision making is not encouraged calmly ask the following question: What would you rather, potentially going three steps back but definitely moving up to 10 steps forward? Or making no steps forward at all?

And if that doesn't get them thinking, then you need to look at moving on to another team or organisation where your ability to make decisions will be recognised, supported and rewarded.

Coping with indigestion?

Q: What if I trust my staff and they make a decision that empties out my bank account?

A: *It is your judgement call about the responsibilities afforded to each employee. Do you give a junior admin clerk the codes to authorise a £1m budget spend? Of course not. It is YOUR responsibility to set the parameters within which an employee can behave. But once you have you must trust them to do their job and take and implement decisions that are related to their role and that side of the business.*

Q: But how do I trust them but monitor them at the same time?

A: *Again, this comes down to the internal systems and processes you have in place. Regular one to ones and team meetings THAT ARE TWO WAY are a must and yet it something many managers pay lip service to so in the end they try to micromanage their employees and waste enormous amounts of time and resources doing so, whilst also creating learned helplessness.*

Part Two:

The 12 Principles of Success

Okay, we've done the preparations and the aromas are starting to whet your appetite. Now it's time for the main course. So have a drink, grab your knife and fork and get ready to tuck in.

Principle 1.
The Caduceus Principle!
Prevention is better than the cure!

It's an old cliché and yet it has become so embedded within our psyche that we ignore it. And to do so is rather stupid because as clichés go, it's one of the most practically helpful ones.

The Caduceus rod has long become synonymous with medical practitioners and if the medical world teaches us nothing it teaches us that it's easier and cheaper to prevent disease occurring than trying to treat it later! But thinking about what to cut is completely the wrong focus! [44]

---

[44] The caduceus is actually the traditional symbol of Hermes, and features two snakes around an often winged staff. It is mistakenly used as a symbol of medicine instead of the Rod of Asclepius, especially in the United States of America. The two-snake caduceus design has ancient and consistent associations with commerce, eloquence, trickery and negotiation. Association of the caduceus with medicine can be traced to the Renaissance, where it was often associated with alchemy and wisdom. The modern use of the caduceus as a symbol of medicine became established in the United States in the late 19th and early 20th century as a result of confusion. I am keeping it here because it has now become such an associated image.

As organisations and as individuals, we must constantly expand our horizons. The best way to grow, to be successful, to stay ahead of the game, is to constantly learn new skills and enhance our knowledge. Why is it therefore that the first two things businesses believe that they must cut during hard times are the marketing and training budgets!?! Ladies and gentlemen: these are the very TWO things that are needed more than ever to keep your company ahead of the competition.

For government, councils and statutory agencies, marketing budgets are a nonsense of course (although I do see local councils, agencies and government departments embarking on such idiotic ventures[45]), but the training budget, ah well, that's something entirely different.

Now, we've already discussed the idea of *waste not want not* in the book, what we're going to focus on here is that cutting back on your staff's ability to improve their skills, and your marketing department's ability to promote exactly how those improved skills keep you ahead of the competition in being able to better support your clients, may not be the best form of prevention out there.

So why do our management teams (and government ministers) instantly think that the only way out of a financial mess is to cut anything that moves. In the UK, local councils in particular are being told: do more with less than you currently have. And there are ways to do this. But it's going to take individual will to make it happen because the most effective way of doing this goes against the deeply embedded belief (mostly subconscious but often conscious too!) in the UK that the management team must have total control over their workforce. This same management team cry foul to the national Government about the enforcements of cuts, but then enforce arbitrary cuts on their own services and staff. They too have become used to being in charge, making all the decisions and expecting them to be carried out like commands from a General in war time.

---

[45] I am not talking about marketing a new community service, I am talking about promoting themselves as being a great council/department/agency.

This is also how private businesses behave. Look where that behaviour has got us. Now don't get me wrong, sometimes one has to look at fat and waste and trim it somewhat to stay lean and energetic. But we become obsessed with cutting and because we are obsessed, that's what we focus on. And we forget that we also need to be increasing revenues, market shares, keeping our employees on side and our customers happy.

No, there are ways to reduce operational costs whilst improving the ability of employees to effectively do their work. One way is to start to adapt our model of working and break from the traditional 9-5 approach that breeds conformity and little else.

In other words, we should use this time to be trying new ways of generating new income and becoming more efficient. To return to our medical theme: if we cut too deep without keeping the blood supply flowing, we will kill the patient.

WELCOME TO THE WORLD OF THE REAL

Of course, if we followed the idea of waste not want not and this principle of prevention is better than cure during the good times, a lot of the pain we're feeling now wouldn't actually be around. Unfortunately we haven't and we do, so what can we learn from this?[46]

We should learn that the same level of thinking that has got us this far is now to blame for the mess we're in. Things need to change. But what should we change?

One thing we should change is how we value our employees. For example, statutory agencies, businesses and Government in GB PLC (and USA Corp, and France Ltd etc) need to welcome in a whole new world of work practices in which we:

---

[46] This is my instant question whenever I make a mistake or affected by external occurrences.

a) Reward our employees for taking the pain that many are currently taking.
b) Make them feel supported in, and encouraged to make, contributions to the success of the organisation.
c) Appreciate the skills and knowledge our employees possess and maximise their ability to push those skills to their ultimate potential.

These employees then start to become part of a bank of assets that will benefit your organisation hugely. The core of these assets is what is known as "knowledge workers."

While such terms don't convey the subtleties of such a new style of workplace, it does identify its most exciting feature: knowledge and skills rule, and these resources must be owned by the individual, not by the company. With this ownership individuals forge new opportunities for work that is more challenging, fun, and self-expressive. But organisations, by acknowledging and supporting the employee in his or her knowledge quest, forge new opportunities for enhanced service delivery- and new ways of working and service thinking too. "Skills," business guru Tom Peters proclaimed as far back as 2001, "are liberating as Hell!"

In effect it creates a positive feedback loop: the organisation creates an environment that supports the employee in being able to utilise their skills and knowledge; the knowledge worker feels able to use that knowledge to the benefit of the organisation; the organisation benefits from a new idea or efficiency and in turn rewards the knowledge worker by allowing them to progress to the next level of thinking; the knowledge worker feels able to use that thinking to the benefit of the organisation... and so on and so on.

Yet, in this country at least, we resist empowering our employees too much- we refuse to allow training and up-skilling on the basis of "we pay, the person trains and then goes to another company!" The argument misses the point: if we create highly skilled, knowledgeable and motivated individuals, it is up to how WE manage them that creates the reward. Simply expecting the newly skilled individual to go about business as usual will indeed make them look elsewhere for satisfaction. I've even seen (nay, experienced!) organisations attempt to stifle such knowledge and ability instead of allowing free expression, maintaining the status quo rather than enabling dynamic change.

Control it seems, in the UK at least, is all.

Words of Wisdom

"The things we fear most in organizations - fluctuations, disturbances, imbalances - are the primary sources of creativity." Margaret J. Wheatley

Another new perception of how we could be working is what author Daniel Pink calls 'Free Agent Nation' in a book by that name. While the near future is not likely to consist solely of independent workers, we are moving towards a world in which most people work like free agents. Or, as Pink puts it, "we're all going Hollywood." Mimicking the film industry talent assembles with talent to complete a project, and then quickly disperses and moves onto the next project. Certainly, most of my business at the moment is coming from joint venture working where other companies- many of them also new businesses- seek to employ my skills as part of their overall project offering.

Tom Peters calls it 'Project World' - a place in which a career is "a portfolio of projects that teach you new skills... grow your colleague set, and constantly reinvent you as a brand." The trick is enabling such a world to exist as much within organisations, and for employees, as it does for freelancers.

For individuals, there are ramifications too: while this rapidly changing, 'free agent' labour market gives individuals more control over their careers, it also means they need to constantly update their skills. The kind of security that one was scared to give up - working for one company for a lifetime - no longer exists anyway and we have to reassess security in the light of Stan Davis & Christopher Meyer's assertion that "the kind of security you're looking for most likely lies in your own skill base and how you wield it in the open marketplace".

However, in a rapidly changing, skills- based economy, as Tom Peters bluntly states, "we are RAPIDLY depreciating assets." To avoid 'depreciation,' individuals must become a lifelong learner, updating skills multiple times per year. Dan Pink observed that "in the newly liberated world of work, it's diversify or die."

Take a bite...

Most organisations have a customer satisfaction survey, but how many have a staff satisfaction survey? Very few. If you don't know how your workforce is feeling how can you properly maintain high levels of effectiveness? You can't. So organise a survey, make sure it is completely anonymous and presented as such. Don't just ask closed questions; leave room for employees to make comments, suggestions and criticisms. If you're in need of making cutbacks, ask THEM for ideas on how to become more efficient and don't just pay lip service to the results. Just the reality of this process will increase the bond between employee and organisation.

Of course, skills, or the implementation of knowledge, will only liberate individuals who can demonstrate them. In response to this need, the past 15 years or so (in the private sector that is) is witness to an explosion in skill certification offerings. Yet companies are being left behind because of this resistance to a shift in working power. We are told that we must move from a world of conformity, loyalty, and hierarchy to one of entrepreneurship, mobility, and fluidity- and certainly this latter aspect is one that the UK Government espouses. Entrepreneurs will save the day they proclaim!

Yet I'm not too sure that these same political and business masters (let's face it, most of the Government are so tied up in big business that there is little distinction) are ready to confront the first part of that statement. In effect, they want the "entrepreneurship, mobility, and fluidity" without the "move from a world of conformity, loyalty, and hierarchy", but haven't realised that the pursuance of one- especially in the context of getting workers to do more with less, is a logical progression of the other.

Power may however be shifting from the organisation to the individual in a subtle, unexpected and negative way: we, as individuals, have realised that our boss won't look after us when times get tough. So why should we be loyal in return? Once we ask that question, we move logically to asking what is it that we can do to make ourselves as secure as possible, and that may mean taking our skills and knowledge elsewhere.

As the factors that have caused this shift - global competition, technological innovation, deregulation, the banking crisis - intensify, we can expect to see individuals push to gain more control in the future. This will cause increasing tensions everywhere because the political and financially elite don't want that kind of chaos. I mean, the more we build our knowledge and skills, the less likely we're going to do as we're told, or believe it when a minister next answers a question with "what people need to understand is that we inherited.... etc." Even our school system is built on the principle of orderly control, turning out little robots who learn their programs (by rote) so that they can be good little factory workers. Or its modern equivalent: the call centre scriptee.

For the UK alone, such entrenched resistance to change could have serious ramifications on the future economic growth of the country on a global stage. It will be those organisations (whether local Government, Government departments, statutory agencies or businesses) who both accept and adapt the principle of building and retaining knowledge workers who succeed because such individuals will drive forward growth (or enhanced or more productive services) through innovation.

In other words, the prevention strategy here is to shore up your knowledge base, both as an organisation and as an individual.

Which is why the training budget should not be cut. Refocused maybe.

But cut?

Nah.

Try something else...

Closely related to this idea of prevention being better than the cure, is Principle 6: The Unexpected Guest. Combining these two principles alone will enable you to head off many potential issues.

Principle 1: The Caduceus Principle in Summary.

Prevention is better than the cure but choose your tactics carefully. There are many alternatives to facing hard times than simply making cuts in expenditure and resources. In the end it comes down to what you would prefer to take: tonic or medicine.

Coping with indigestion?

Q: I agree with what you are saying here. Be a good organisation, develop your staff, let them create - be successful. Be a good worker, learn and develop, help the organisation grow - be successful. It is critical to economic development in the longer term. However, training budgets are often wasted. Training courses are often very poor, very expensive and very poorly

targeted in terms of who attends. What can we do to make sure any expenditure won't it will be a big waste of resources?

A: *I agree entirely. Some of the problem stems from "training" money being conditional on tick boxes being ticked, which focuses the mind on the wrong aspect, i.e. the process rather than the people. Another is the fact that often the people commissioning the training don't know enough about training, or the subject needed to be taught etc so just believe what they're told/charged by the training company. Training budgets should not be stopped, but the way that they are administered should be drastically changed.*

Principle 2

The Maverick Principle!

Don't shoot the messenger. Embrace him instead!

Our natural instinct when someone questions what we're doing is to defend our position. When someone appears to completely ignore rules we get even more irate. But in doing so we miss the point: why is this person being challenging?

Definition of Maverick: One who refuses to abide by the dictates of his group; a dissenter! So says the Readers Digest so it must be true. But Mavericks should not be classed as trouble makers but rather as a valuable asset that can help your business become more robust and exciting.

Ladies and gentlemen.

For those of you who regularly read my blogs, or know me personally, this won't come as a surprise, but I have a confession to make. I am a maverick. Well, at least this is what I am told- mostly by ex-bosses and good friends. It's true to say that I have always asked difficult questions, sought to cut through the bull, thumped desks in difficult meetings to stop bickering egos and clans, and come up with off the wall projects and concepts to get things done.

And, it doesn't matter how high up the food chain you are, if I think you're wrong, I'll tell you that you are- first of all explaining why I think you're wrong, and then showing you how to put it right.

So, if all that makes me a maverick, then hands up.

To me, being a maverick is to be someone who sees things differently from what is accepted to be the norm, and then have a compulsion to challenge things if they perceive what they see to be wrong, or can be made better.

Now, and this is in my experience, *ALL* organisations say that they want people to challenge the way things are done if they can be done better. In fact, in interviews I have made it clear that I am that person who will look to challenge you in the "why are we doing things this way" front and have been hired on that basis!

However, the reality is that once on board mavericks are then expected to follow the rules- both the explicit and implicit ones.

For example, in an interview with a local council, I was explaining my approach to dealing with turf protectors. I will patiently define what a shovel is to you three times. If you still refuse to accept the definition, I will hit you on the head with it. In other words, I will try to work with you on a problem, project or resource exchange three times, after that, if you still refuse to engage in the process because you simply want to protect your interests, I will go around, over or through you. The executive interviewing me and who would ultimately be my boss, said, "Would that include me if I was getting in the way too?" Absolutely I answered. I got the job. I was told that my focus on getting the job done even if it meant using extreme tactics to get around people resistant to the new way of partnership working, was one of the main reasons I did so.

Imagine my surprise therefore that when a senior executive at a partner organisation was doing exactly that, blocking initiatives and in fact stealing resources away from the project that she was supposed to be supporting, and I openly criticised her for doing so, I was summarily hung out to dry. What was very satisfying for me to watch unfold over the following year however was how much the balance of power swung to her away from the management team who did not make a stand against her on my behalf. They had run for cover, not wanting to be seen by people further up the tree to be rocking the boat.

In doing so, they had missed the point of my rebellion. Things were not good in Denmark. In fact they were rotten. The project I was supporting therefore became a shadow of its former self and no longer really delivers any benefit other than keeping a few brown noses in work.

Words of Wisdom

"There are no foolish questions, and no man becomes a fool until he has stopped asking questions." Anthony Robbins

In reality therefore, a maverick is slammed down on, told to shut up, disciplined, even fired- simply for doing the very things that organisations say they want their staff to do!

This misses the point of a maverick. Mavericks will create new ways of working, they will stop you from stagnation, they will create excitement and passion, and they will ALWAYS be looking for ways to improve things- everything - about your business or organisational effectiveness.

Again, I can point to massive successes when organisations have used my work- sometimes reluctantly or in a period of time after I've been gone and they think no-one will notice the work being passed off as belonging to someone else. For example- you want a new way of engaging with communities, before SNTs[47] were even floated in the Casey Report- see the 3 tier model of engagement adopted years later as best practice by Casey (but sadly never really implemented properly- too much power left with the police). You want to involve communities more in managing local resources whilst reducing Council bills, see the Community Asset Management Framework & Impact Assessment Process and the Young People Area Assembly models created in the summer of 2007, the former now finally adopted by a local council but put out under someone else's name (the same council have also won awards and hard cash for my work on the YPAA). You want a new way of raising sustainable revenues (from businesses) without spending a lot of money- see the ITu series which gave away information and strategies about technology coming on stream that could help clients but never sold the company I was working for at the time.

And so on- it doesn't matter that I'm not explaining what these initiatives are here, it is sufficient to know that all these came out of my questioning the way things were done and coming up with something completely different. ALL organisations I have worked for have benefited massively from their contributions- even though I have sometimes been bullied, harassed, sullied, shut out and openly criticised.

Just imagine what could have been achieved if those managers who put so much energy into controlling me had been willing to support me instead?

Good job I don't let my shyness or frail ego get in the way.

Seriously, I am not saying all this to say look at me and how brilliant I am (I have made way too many mistakes for that!). The point is, is that somewhere in your organisation is a maverick just bursting with new

---

[47] Safer Neighbourhood Partnership teams, bringing together police, wardens, housing officers and other agencies under one roof to tackle neighbourhood issues.

ideas and concepts and ways of doing things- you need to find them and use them in a positive fashion and NOT shut them up.

Take a bite...

Take a moment to think back to when someone, maybe even you, challenged an established way of doing things, or some new initiative, and suggested a better way or improvement in how to do it- and were shut down. Then think about what the overall result was of not making those changes, or extrapolate out what could be the benefit if the suggested changes are made.

Don't get me wrong here, one shouldn't confuse a maverick with a busybody troublemaker, who is about challenging everything just for the sake of it; or a negative corporate sociopath, that is someone who is all about what makes them look great and death and destruction to everyone else who gets in their way. No, a maverick is someone who wants the business/organisation/team/project to succeed and is willing to do everything humanly possible to make it so!

What should be done therefore is to make sure that you create a culture where mavericks are given the freedom to dig around, challenge managers and executives, burst through barriers with ideas and concepts, and given charge of making change happen. True, you may have to remind them every now and again to watch their Ps & Qs as passion can sometimes reduce social skill, but trust me, if you've got a maverick in your team and you're not allowing them free rein, you're going to always do what's expected of you, rather than get people wondering how the heck you've managed to achieve everything you've done!

I am a big believer in using questions to move forward- whether in life, business or indeed arguments of a political nature. Apparently, I'm always in trouble with our political masters because I do demand answers, or will point out when things are not right (I do point out alternative strategies by the way, I don't just say that's rubbish!).

For a time, it used to get me down that I would have my knees chopped off for merely asking "why are we doing this?", but this is just stupid. I've now worked out that, actually, I don't care about their insults, manipulations, rubbish-him campaigns as they don't hurt nearly as much as not being true to oneself. As Tom Peters said, "If no-one is pissed off with you, then you're already dead and just haven't figured it out yet."

So, be kind to a maverick soon. The payback will be worth it, trust me.

Try something else...

Help your mavericks express their true selves by implementing Principle 5: The Round Table Principle.

Principle 2: The Maverick Principle in Summary.

Having people who question your thinking, processes and systems, especially whilst making suggestions and putting forward new ideas means that you get to test those systems for robustness. These are the rebels in the FDG and you need them.

Coping with indigestion?

Q: Isn't letting someone question what you're doing showing weakness?

A: It depends on how you handle it. I had one boss who would listen to what I had to say. If he thought there was anything in it, he would explore it further. If he disagreed with my assessment, he would say so but then explain why he disagreed.

Even if I still disagreed with his reasons, the fact that he had listened, noted what I said and then explained (not dictated) why his decision should stand, was enough to make sure I did everything I could to make that the existing process/procedure/campaign worked to the best possible outcome. I think the weakness comes from shutting people down and playing the "I'm the boss you do as I say" card; remember, people need to feel that they are valued.

Principle 3

The Jewish Vampire Principle!
Right tools and people for the right job!

Ever wonder why in all the vampire films and TV series that it is the crucifix that seems to ward off the fanged menaces? It took a crazy 1980s comedy movie called Hysterical, which had a Jewish Count Dracula simply yawn at the heroes attempt to frighten him off with a cross, to make me realise that actually, a crucifix really would not work on a Jewish (or Muslim or Atheist etc) Vampire.[48]

It's another one of those cliché doubles that everyone knows about but don't actually stop to take in: One size fits/doesn't fit all! Yet how many services or products are designed with one design template in mind, usually the one that is based on the beliefs, likes and traits of the person designing it?

---

[48] Buffy the Vampire Slayer came up with its own unique solution: Vampires were from a hell dimension that inhabited the bodies of their victims in this dimension and their fear of the cross was due to it been a symbol of power in their original dimension. Clever, eh?

Back in the 1980s, Faith Popcorn and the Brain Reserve, a kind of funky future envisioning organisation, predicted the rise of customised products and services. For a while, it seemed as though her model of design and delivery was going to be spot on the button; pizzas could be ordered with different toppings on the same base, ice creams came in a whole host of flavours via Ben & Jerry's, bikes could have different accessories, cars and computers could be designed around a core chassis and Burger King told us we would have it our way.

But something happened. Somewhere, the commercial advantage of being able to offer tailored services got lost in the quest for instant profits and therefore pharmaceutical companies, banks and financial institutions, energy companies and utility companies swamped us with so many different choices and types of tariff that simply meant we weren't able to choose the most effective solution for us. In other words, these companies purposely used choice to mean that the consumer wasn't able to truly choose the best option for them!

Worse, the basic service world, including many local government agencies across the world, hid behind financial pressures and the mess the big corporations got into, to effectively say: this is our solution, make it fit you.

For example, in the UK, the last two or three governments have pushed the e-government agenda. The idea behind it was a simple and valid one: use the economies of scale and ease of use of the internet to reduce costs, help the public (or local business) conduct their day to day interactions (e.g. pay their rates) and combine back office function with real time service delivery.

Words of Wisdom

"Oy vey, have you got the wrong vampire." Shagal, the Inn-Keeper, as a young woman tries to fend off Shagail, a Jewish Vampire, with a cross.

Now, young people may well be hip to using smart phones and iPADS and antiquated laptops (isn't that a scary thought that many young people look at traditional IT devices as *so yesterday*?) but many old people simply don't have access to them, or the skills to use them. Many even need the human contact provided at that payment office to break up days of solitude.

Now, I love e-systems. I really do. When used correctly they can save users time and companies/organisations money- in fact lots of both. So when the last government said it was going to develop e-gov services and force local authorities to do the same (remember "joined up government"??) I applauded. At last thought I, a quick and efficient way to get service.

Unfortunately many local authorities and government departments either don't understand how to roll out e-gov OR see it as a way to either put barriers between them and those pesky members of the public, or as a means to cut costs without really improving service. Worse, e-services are being designed by people who just don't understand the needs of their clients.

So your systems must always be created with the user/customer/client in mind. If they're not, you're failing the very people who you depend on to be successful, and all for the sake of saving a few thousand pounds. Let me give you a prime example.

A friend of mine has a son- let's call him Robert- who is both autistic, and learning disabled. No, the two don't mean the same thing. He is however a determined young man, who is educating himself, trying to live independently and has an ambition to have a career in music. But for all that, there are certain fundamentals that he finds impossible to comprehend and others that are extremely difficult to learn. For example, money from the bank machine was just "free" money for the longest time- he simply didn't get the concept of money going in must be greater than money going out (although I often find that concept difficult to follow too).

Likewise, sending letters and forms and emails regarding service provision, service charges and so on that are your box standard letter template would just cause confusion and in some cases panic. Worse still, he and his mother (who is principle carer) still get letters saying that he must submit to an almost annual review of his condition to see if he's better now and therefore shouldn't be receiving this benefit or other. Hello Mr Beaurocrat-Sat-In-An-Office-Designing-Processes-For-People-He-Is-Not-Qualified-To-Assess: *autism doesn't get better or spontaneously cure itself!!!* You're wasting money and creating unnecessary stress on individuals so that you can tick a box. Or because you simply don't know the reason why the individual is on benefits in the same place because nothing on your log in page connects to other services.

And this brings me to the point of e-gov and joined up government. Robert is autistic. He has had numerous assessments, reviews and treatment meetings. Why then doesn't a little flag pop up when Mr B thinks it's time to have a review? Surely social services, medical records, benefits records should all be linked by now? No? Oh.

But it gets worse.

Rob needed to renew his bus pass. A simple thing you would think, apart from he didn't understand the standard reminder that was sent to him. Now, remember, Rob is doing a full time course so that he can get a paid job and support himself: a bus pass is therefore essential. So when eventually he realises he needs a new one he speaks to his mum who takes time out of the office to go to the local SYPTE office. This is supposed to be the combined transport-local authority-business organisation: one service front combining the resources of multiple organisations.

Rob waits in line at the SYPTE office only to be told that he can't have a replacement until he has proof from the local authority that he should have one. Mum says but you sent a reminder saying he needs to renew his pass. Well says the operative, its procedure, we have to follow procedure and procedure says we have to have a letter from social services and the council verifying he can have a bus pass. Mum asks can't you just check online? No says the operative, we're not linked into the council's system. Hmmmm.

So mum and Rob go to where they are sent. Mum is by now past her allocated lunch time. As they walk in to this other office a sign says "Learning Disabled Go To Main Reception" (or words to this effect)- so they queue, only to be told that they need in fact to go to a different floor.

When they get there it is packed with people waiting for "non-learning disabled" services so mum thinks hang on a minute they said to go to main reception and main reception is where we're going. Main reception don't like the fact that Rob & mum reappear and demand to be seen as the notice says but agree to call upstairs to get an answer on the phone.

There is a mumbled conversation. Main reception then shouts out across the reception area- "Is it learning disabled???" Yes sighs mum, wondering where treating everyone with respect has gone to in this moment as people in reception stare at Rob.

There's more mumbled conversation, the upshot of which is: Rob has to get a letter confirming he is learning disabled and autistic from his doctor (again, because even though he had a letter last year there is of course a chance that his autism has cured itself after all. No, *really*.). The help desk will then ask Social Services to verify this and will then write to SYPTE saying Rob is eligible for a pass.

Are we losing the will to live yet?

Mum and Rob comply and go back a few days later. There's still forms and stuff to do of course. Mum asks the question (as Rob hasn't the faintest idea really of what is going on but is stressed at being in queues again)- why can't you all just link up into one system, or at least have social services and the helpdesk linked up into a central record system?

Ah says the helpdesk, we can't do that because we're actually not council frontline staff, we're a private company subcontracted by the council to deliver public service on their behalf. But we can't have access to their record system because of data protection.

So, to recap: to get a renewed bus pass, Rob needed to involve his doctor, SYPTE, social services, the council AND a third party private company. Not a single one of whom were linked electronically. And yet this is the same council who has made it impossible for the public to pay for certain services except via e-gov portals and is insistent that e-gov is the way forward.

Might I make a suggestion? Might the services actually implement e-gov internally first, across partners second and then lastly, when all the services are indeed joined up, implement e-service for the masses? Or am I being too simplistic?

WHAT DOES ALL THIS TELL US ABOUT RIGHT TOOLS?

In other words, driving to hit a target that 85% of all rates payments and enquiries should be completed on the internet by the end of 2020 is another example of hitting the target but missing the point. It may well reduce your costs for delivering a customer service, but isn't customer service supposed to be a lot more than simply providing a quick and easy way for some customers to be able to pay?

Private businesses often behave no better. All I will say here is: phone menu systems. You can try telling us all you want that the menu system on your public service line is there to "better direct us to where we need to be" for our query "to be more effectively handled", but the reality is NONE OF YOUR CUSTOMERS LIKE IT and few even think the reasons you give for implementing the system are even true. So why do you persist? Because the service you are pushing is homogenised and cheaper for you to run. Be honest. Tell the truth; at least you'd get brownie points from customers who have the misfortune to call. And don't go complaining either that there is no customer loyalty anymore.

Take a bite...

Personally test every aspect of a new streamlined service that your organisation has put in place. For the purpose of this chew, we'll say the new phone menu system your company has installed to more effectively handle your (as the customer) call. Does it make you feel frustrated? Do you ever get into endless loop syndrome?[49] Do you sometimes not find the option you need and have to guess which one is best fit? Is your option to speak to a human representative the last option given? If so, tear it up and start again. Same with e-systems, appointment systems, purchasing systems and so on. If they have not been designed for the customer, get rid of them[50].

But we shouldn't just think about processes and systems here, you need to think about your people placement too. Old Genghis might be absolutely brilliant in your environmental law enforcement department, and be one of the most respected executives you've got. That does not make him the right leader to put in place to take charge of your emergency & disaster response centre should an unexpected flood occur. You need someone who can make fast, tactical decisions true, but you also need someone who can empathise with the families affected by the floods, so that the decisions just don't get the job done of saving lives, but take care of the immediate emotional needs of the survivors too (especially the very young).

We spent a great deal of Focus Area 14 talking about the right person for the right job, so we won't labour the point here.

---

[49] By the way, any company that I use where the phone menu system ends up taking me right back to where I started 20 options ago is automatically removed as a personal service provider at the first opportunity. Maybe I should start listing them on my website too.

[50] Again, see Patricia Seybold's books for great roadmaps of implementation.

Try something else...

Go back to Focus Area 14: Right Person for The Right Job and think about how you choose your people placement, product design and service delivery.

In conclusion then, the purpose of this principle is to get you to move away from the 'one size fits all' concept, but not just from accepting that 'one size doesn't fit all' point of view. You have to design every aspect of your business with your clients in mind. They have individual needs wrapped up within those generic market segmentations.

Suffice it to say that going into battle against the forces of evil armed with only one form of religious sacrament may not be the best policy to follow.

Principle 3: The Jewish Vampire Principle in Summary.

Don't design your products, services or internal processes without thinking about the needs of your clients.

Coping with indigestion?

Q: But we can save huge costs by streamlining our phone access system. Surely that's a good thing?

A: *It is if it doesn't drive customers away. Streamlining costs is all well and good so long as the process doesn't also reduce your income coming in. I am not saying that you shouldn't look at making systems more efficient, rather that you must always look at the possible impact of those efficiency savings on the client and his or her negative view of the company, whether or not that new view is perception or reality.*

Principle 4

The Court Jester Principle!

You're having a laugh! If not, why not?

IN a 7 day period you spend around 112 hours awake. Of that you spend around 40 hours at work, and 10 hours travelling to and from work. If you're not happy at work, you're losing almost half of your waking hours in a mire of getting through the day.

There are some managers who think that if their staff are laughing then work is not being done. I know that isn't you, but I bet you can recognise other managers who do. But what would you rather: a happy workforce who enjoy being at work, or a set of moaners who can't wait to get home?

John Cleese, the former Monty Python in charge of funny walks, coined it correctly when he said: *You don't have to be sombre to be serious.* Think about that statement for a moment. What does it actually mean?

Whilst you're thinking, I will continue by saying that I have a reputation as being a wise ass. I come out with the one liners, I don't take authority particularly seriously unless I believe they have earned the right (so when you tell me you're the President of XYZ Corp don't expect me to treat you any differently from the receptionist who probably works harder and knows more about what's going on in XYZ Corp than you do!), and I challenge, tease and harass with good humour some of your most embedded belief systems. I've been called everything from a joker, to a trouble maker, to a maverick (mostly this actually), to someone who asks too many questions, to being a complete rebel. And a number of plain insults too.

But I also have a reputation for being someone who gets the job done, who takes charge in difficult situations, for being uniquely creative, who goes the extra mile, who provides service over and above, and who is able to cut through all the bull and come up with the necessary solution.

The problem is that most of the managers who know I belong in the second category set can't get their heads around that I also belong in the first set of categories. They simply cannot see the link between the two. I get my energy and creative flow from asking questions, having fun, looking for new ways of doing things.

So why can't they see this? Why can't some managers understand that mocking your staff for having a chat, or laughing together, is actually NOT a great thing for their business?

A POSSIBLE BELIEF SYSTEM THAT SAYS WE SHOULDN'T BE LAUGHING AT WORK

A few years ago I was listening to the BBC debate following David Cameron's speech at his party conference and the whole focus was on the idea that we should reward those who get up at the crack of dawn and go to work. The overall message is, as always in the UK, "be productive". It is, it would seem, a patriotic duty to be producing away, to be working all the hours one can. Sleep is for wimps. Lunch is for wimps. Let's get back to that 80's culture where we all should succeed no matter what the cost!

Perhaps you subscribe to this thinking. If you do, let me issue a wakeup call:

- It was the 80s that created the banking system and greed that led us to the current disaster.
- It was the 80s that created the idea of me-me-me over society, community and responsibility that has seen such a massive breakdown in respect and morality in this country.
- It was through the 80s culture of work until you drop that has led to the world's unhappiest workforce, the blurring of work-home balance, and the worst family cohesion set up in the western world[51].

And all this is what has led to where we are today. Because we never stopped being driven to produce. All our work related systems, our education systems and our government systems are locked into this obsession. Remember the organisation I worked for recently that gave me a Blackberry programmed to come on at 6am, go off at midnight, or come on at any time should an email be sent by the boss?

I may well have had the skill to reprogram it, but that's not the point. It's the assumption that the management had the right to do this because it maximised *productivity* that is the issue.

This obsession will crush the UK in the long run. It is the living example of the woodsman too busy to sharpen his saw and wondering why it is taking longer and longer, and being more exhaustive, to cut down the tree[52].

So what's the solution? Simple. Change our obsession with "productivity" into an obsession about "contribution". No, the two things are *not* the same.

---

[51] More or less. Go do the research- hey, I'm not here to do everything for you!

[52] Yes I know I keep pushing this analogy but as they say, repetition is the mother of skill and eventually you'll start to work with this concept rather than just know it.

Being productive means we must have something to show that can be measured in hard currency. The hours worked; the outputs/physical products produced; the number of qualifications gained; the number of staff answering emails from their boss at 2am and so on.

Words of Wisdom

"Unless each day can be looked back upon by an individual as one in which he has had some fun, some joy, some real satisfaction, that day is a loss." Dwight D Eisenhower

Being contributory means something completely different. It is more a focus on giving something- an idea, a skill, a service, a little help. It can be about developing a business or generating hard cash for sure, but it also lends itself much more to getting that community green cleared out so that young people can play there, or giving your time to visiting old folk and engaging them in discussions about their life, or simply taking time out and writing that song/book/poem that will affect someone, somewhere at some time on an emotional or intellectual level, or even generate a light-bulb moment that could change the world. Or even giving time to your family so your child feels loved, supported, listened to and respected. What could be more important in the whole world than that?

Being productive means we have no time, we simply do.

Being contributory means we take time to be *and* do.

That's why we talked about running work like a social club, so that everyone, including you, feels like getting up on any kind of morning and coming to work, where they feel happy and supported, view their colleagues as buddies and, above all, really feel like they are achieving something. And people feel a much more heightened sense of achievement if they believe they have made a contribution rather than just produced something to tick a box. So let's lose the obsession with being productive and concentrate on what's really important.

Take a bite...

Next time you hear your staff having a discussion or laughing, don't walk up and admonish or even offer a quiet tut as you walk by. Instead, listen for a moment and if you catch the drift, join in. If you don't catch the drift, or don't have anything to add, simply walk on by with a smile.

Even if you don't agree that the obsession with productivity (or targets) is why our management teams frown on people being funny or chatty at work, you must admit that there is a culture of frowning. Another possible reason for this is that we are taught that there must be a cultural divide between management and work force, a boundary so to speak that guides the interaction. Plus we also fall into that trap of those managers who simply don't know how to manage and believe that their role is to dictate, rather than offer support, to their staff.

It never ceases to amaze me that the benefits of having a happy workforce must be obvious to all (and studies over the years have shown what these benefits are; see Manpower studies from over a decade ago for example!) and yet many managers still find it impossible to stop themselves from being all big boss. To those managers I say you must work on your ability to laugh at yourself, and to relate to the people you manage. Only then will you start to see real and sustainable 'productivity' gains. To then go through the roof, remove the obsession about productivity gains and focus instead on what contribution can you and your team/department/organisation really start to make. The "productivity" will then occur naturally and as a positive consequence of what you are doing, rather than it being a forced set of activities due to a focus on ticking those boxes.

Try something else...

Go back to Focus Area 5: Play Nice and think about how you work with your work force or team.

Principle 4: The Court Jester Principle in Summary.

You must create an environment in which you and your team look forward to coming into work because you have fun, contribute and feel valued.

Coping with indigestion?

Q: If I let people simply chat all day how does that benefit the company?

A: *Okay, let's be clear. There are people, as we've said, who will slope off. Your job as a manager in this context is to separate out the ones who simply take any opportunity to have a natter as a way of not doing work, from those who are taking a break from working and having a laugh with a colleague. Not only do you benefit from having a relaxed work force who feel like they are treated like adults, studies also show that when someone takes a conscious break from an activity (as opposed to an external interruption) they return to it (or ready to start a new activity) refreshed and with more energy and creativity.*

If you can't be bothered to research the studies on the web, try this approach on yourself. Start taking short breaks between activities to make a cup of tea or read a chapter from a book or go for a quick walk around the building (in other words, something not directly work related- no, answering emails doesn't count!) and see how more effective you are when you return back to the task.

Principle 5

The Round Table Principle!

Bad news must travel fast! Useful ideas must travel faster.

If you have a suggestions box do you actively review the suggestions posted? Do you even have a suggestion box in the first place? If not, you're missing out on crucial pieces of information.

You have your intranet and email systems. You pump out the usual corporate information, working policies, news and announcements and even promote the annual company ball. But you simply aren't realising the huge potential of these platforms!

The Round Table principle is probably the biggest and most complicated of all the ideas in this book in terms of the initial cost and effort it will require getting it established. It is also the principle that if fully understood and implemented will bring the biggest benefits to any organisation.

There are two primary elements to the Round Table Principle:

1. The idea that everyone connected to your organisation is vital to your organisation's success
2. To contribute to that success they must be provided with the tools and processes to do so.

My thinking behind The Round Table Principle arose from an almost desperate strategy forged in the 1990s when Microsoft came up with the idea of The Digital Nervous System.

THE DIGITAL NERVOUS SYSTEM AND THE ROUND TABLE PRINCIPLE.

In the mid-1990s, just as IBM's continued investment in their OS/2 operating system platform was finally starting to pay dividends- and the long awaited Microsoft Windows 4 and NT 5 were once again delayed, Bill Gates began formulating his concept of "the digital nervous system" (DNS). Microsoft led so heavily on the idea that corporations were asking where they could "buy this DNS from", but it wasn't until 1999 when Gates crystallised the idea in his book "Business at the speed of thought" that people realised that it wasn't a product at all, but a concept, an ambition that one day might be fulfilled through technology. In effect, and I know Microsoft will deny this but I was there at the time, the DNS was a market spoiler[53] aimed at derailing increasing publicity for IBM's OS/2. But as spoilers go it was a doozy!

The concept behind the DNS is a simple one: anyone in your organisation whether it is the janitor, receptionist, sales director or President, has some kind of skill, contact, and piece of information (even gossip) or experience that can help your organisation. These combine to become the organisation's lifeblood. The DNS therefore is, in the Microsoft context, the technological infrastructure that pumps that lifeblood around. It also includes ideas, suggestions and opportunities for cost reduction as well as sales.

---

[53] Note, I am not saying it was a lie- once thought up, Microsoft developed a serious set of solutions.

It must also include the idea that bad news must travel fast. That is, when something goes wrong, this should be communicated along with the fixes and/or lessons learned by the organisation. We instinctively want to bury bad news, after all we don't want to look bad do we, but a DNS actually allows us to use it as a catalyst for change and improvement. In effect the "immediate availability of accurate information changes strategic thinking from a separate, standalone activity to an on-going process integrated with regular business activities." [54]

Words of Wisdom

During my second year of nursing school our professor gave us a quiz. I breezed through the questions until I read the last one: "What is the first name of the woman who cleans the school?" Surely this was a joke. I had seen the cleaning woman several times, but how would I know her name? I handed in my paper, leaving the last question blank. Before the class ended, one student asked if the last question would count toward our grade. "Absolutely," the professor said. "In your careers, you will meet many people. All are significant. They deserve your attention and care, even if all you do is smile and say hello." I've never forgotten that lesson. I also learned her name was Dorothy. Joann C. Jones

This theme was taken on by other business gurus at the time. Kevin Kelly said: "The concept of a digital nervous system is essentially the implementation, by business users such as you, of wide-reaching computer network and desktop-user connectivity along with deeply integrated insurance-specific computer applications, such as agency management systems, rating products and customer relationship/marketing systems. These next-generation internal systems

---

[54] Bill Gates, Faster Than The Speed of Thought

will deliver on the promise of one of Microsoft's founding missions: "information at your fingertips.""[55]

So how does this relate to The Round Table Principle? Well, the focus of the Digital Nervous System of course was implementing the technological processes that would deliver effective knowledge management to all aspects of your organisation.

What I realised early on however, and which companies around the world came to realise, is that a true DNS is far more than technology. It is no good simply putting in the tools, digital or otherwise, that allow employees to be able to express their useful 'stuff'; you *must* also implement cultural changes that encourage, support and publicly reward them for doing so. After all, some suggestions might be a challenge to the established way of doing things and nothing arouses a manager's ire more than to see their own idea/process being criticised! A true DNS is therefore cultural in nature, and must be embedded within all aspects of the organisation.

Implementing a Round Table Principle culture based around the DNS concept would bring huge benefits to any organisations:

- It can help organisations do several things at the same time.
- It can improve its systems and services by getting real time criticisms, ideas and suggestions fed directly into the weekly staff meetings.
- It raises staff morale by demonstrating that their input is valued.
- It gives staff, suppliers, partners and customers a stake in the success of the business/organisation by not only enabling input but by actively encouraging it.
- It can improve the standing of the establishment locally, politically and nationally because it shows true forward thinking.

---

[55] Kelly, Kevin, *The digital nervous system*. Rough Notes 141. 10 (Oct 1998): 34-36

- It improves the use of ICT within the establishment.

It can also show reduction in costs, improvement in productivity, behaviours and attitudes, and improved uptake of wider initiatives- for example by linking a DNS system into the local community in which your organisation is located.[56]

Furthermore, none of this has to cost a fortune. Technologically speaking, many organisations can utilise their existing technological backbone by developing platforms based on open source software- and early adopters can even expect free support from the likes of Microsoft, IBM etc, all of whom have technological solutions based around the concept of a DNS and who would love to have pilot projects within your establishment.

WHAT ELSE SHOULD WE CONSIDER FOR OUR ROUND TABLE?

There are many different elements you could put into the cultural changes, but one that I would recommend is a principle found within the education world: that of reflecting consistently on evaluation and assessment. Business pedagogy is so firmly entrenched in the notions of capitalism it's often difficult to pull out the nuances of improving through assessment, yet it has long had a focus on skills, professionalism and standards: all these concepts are firmly embedded within the identity of the business community. What the business world may find surprising is that there has been just such a focus by the education community over the last decade or so. So what can the business community learn from this seemingly education based pedagogy? Well, as Paulo Freire says: "Thinking critically about practice,

---

[56] For example in the UK we have what we call The Neighbourhood Learning Net, where ICT usage, tuition and services are provided to members of the community (as well as signposting to wider learning initiatives and opportunities). Unfortunately as I write many of these are being shut down due to cuts.

of today or yesterday, makes possible the improvement of tomorrow's practice".[57]

In the education world, a great deal of time and consideration is given to the pedagogy of learning through assessment, a positive feedback loop approach where you plan, deliver, assess or evaluate and feed your conclusions into the next plan and so on. This is similar to the process of stage evaluations in PRINCE2[58] methodology.

We should also consider that in the teaching world assessment is connected to the individual and what they've learned, whilst evaluation was a judgment about the whole experience; or, as Fisher, Rollin et al define it: "Assessment relates to the measurement and testing of performance; evaluation considers the 'value' or worth of what has taken place. The results of assessment generally inform evaluation."[59]

It is true of course that evaluation has always played an important part in the private and public sectors, but sadly more often than not from a tick the box point of view rather than with any real method of using the evaluation results to feed into a cycle of improvement. It frustrated me incredibly that there would be evaluation forms at the end of seminars but the only thing they were used for was to see how many attendees were satisfied.

For reasons of space we can only discuss two kinds of assessments.

In educational terms, summative assessments take place at the end of the process, designed to find out if the stated learning outcomes have been achieved or the student has achieved a certain grade.

---

[57] Freire, P. (1998). *Pedagogy of freedom: Ethics, democracy, and civic courage*. Lanham, MD: Rowman & Littlefield

[58] PRojects IN a Controlled Environment, the government standard approach to project management

59 James Avis, Roy Fisher, Ron Thompson eds (2010), Teaching in Lifelong Learning, McGraw

Formative assessment takes place during the course, designed to chart the student's development as it progresses. In work terms both these assessment forms could be the objectives agreed during a Personal Development Review (PDR) for example.

Both are more powerful when combined, and then further combined with an initial assessment, or forming of a baseline record of understanding/ability of the individual or group. Assessments can then be referred back to a starting point and a clear progress conclusion reached.

In the business world, I have experienced very little of this kind of approach; that is looking at what has already been done, is planned to be done, assessing internal skills to see if they can be more cost-effectively seconded to a particular project or piece of work. Even the Governments PRINCE2 project management framework insistence on "lessons learned" is largely ignored (which is why so many Government projects appear to have the same fatal issues).

The design and criteria for assessment must be applicable to what you are assessing. Sounds like I'm teaching you to suck eggs but the fact is, I just don't see much *real* assessment conducted. For example, and staying with the education world for a moment, assessing purely theoretical knowledge on a vocational course would miss out key practical and interpersonal skills that may be just as important. Similarly, just providing one kind of assessment may also be counter-productive. This is as true for businesses as anywhere.

Angela Steward points out that;

"... emphasis on the end product of your course may encourage your student to consider anything that is not directly related to this as a waste of time. This narrow focus means students question the relevance of everything they do, which may lead them to underestimate the value of what they bring to the course from outside through their prior experiences and previous education and training. There is a tendency for students to sit passively and rely on you to supply the information that will get them their qualifications."[60]

Take a bite...

Call a meeting with as many people in your organisation that you can muster and have a "Suggestion Box Sandbox". The rules are that everyone has to do one of the following:

1. Suggest some improvement to processes or systems
2. Make a criticism about some aspect of the company or its behaviour that they feel is wrong
3. Talk about some news item or piece of gossip they have heard that relates to the company's marketplace, product set or customer base.
4. Give contact details about someone who could be a potential client, employee or partner.

You should then capture up all these pieces of information and work on them one by one with the group and agree:

1. One action that can be taken against each piece of information
2. Who by and when.
3. When you will all come back together to review progress against the agreed actions.[61]

The business world often misses this point, paying out bonuses to sales people (or bankers) on achievement on narrow revenue targets, failing to monitor (evaluate, assess) the cost of delivering that revenue or

---

[60] Angela Steward (2006), A to Z of Teaching in FE, Continuum

[61] The Inform Group has a whole roadmap of activity that can be conducted beyond the initial "Take a Bite" scenario described above and you should contact our office if you wish to pursue this strategy in detail.

whether or not there are or could be negative implications in achieving that target (as with the financial meltdown). Or the performance management tool becomes one of control. One executive working in local government uses performance appraisal tools to bully, control and ego-stroke himself. In effect, I have seen him leave people in tears or driven out after public humiliation.

The great business leader Tom Peters doesn't miss this point: "In an effort to induce flexibility, we must turn our backs on, or radically redefine, the three staples of control over individuals- performance appraisals, the setting of objectives, and job descriptions... These three control systems, like measurement systems... are increasingly doing more harm than good."[62] That was in 1987. Things are much worse now.

Therefore, assessment must be seen as part of a learning and improvement framework for both learner and provider or employee and company; its purpose must be to collect all types of feedback, whether compliments, criticisms, ideas, suggestions etc. - simply getting a rating on how good you were is not sufficient; a process must be embedded that allows that feedback to be utilised.

An effective assessment process should therefore include planning for assessment; collecting the evidence; making judgments; giving feedback; and recording achievement. There are a couple of caveats to this thinking however. Sometimes, continuous assessments and evaluations can become an almost semi-religious affair, leading to over-planning and/or an obsession with completing the process rather than on the outcome.

This takes the form of:

1. Too much emphasis is placed on the process and not on the outcome. That is, and I saw first hand during my PTTLs course;

---

[62] Tom Peters (1987), Thriving on Chaos: Handbook for a Management Revolution, Macmillan

people were worrying about how to *do* reflective learning rather than learning any lessons from it.
2. All assessments and evaluation techniques, including reflective learning, should include hard looks at mistakes, with support and understanding from the establishment, for the best lessons to be learned.
3. All assessments should produce actions that are followed up. This is such a simple premise and yet missed so easily. The tendency is to posit actions in the reflective essay but then forget all about them.

This is where embedding the concepts of both The Round Table Principle as a cultural focus, and the implementation of a process solution such as a Digital Nervous System (built on whatever platform) can really help. It can use automation to insist on follow-ups (no matter how high up the company someone may be), spread the news instantly, and keep momentum going on dealing with the issues or opportunities that arise out of the initial input.

A DNS based business pedagogy can become a very powerful tool indeed. I have a vision of using DNS technology within a training environment to encourage a DNS culture. Imagine small PDA devices, hooked into a research library, the internet, the intranet and business processes of the establishment delivering or hosting the class, as well as hooked into the individual business student's company intranet and business processes, and into my own knowledge bank here at The Inform Group. The individual can use the PDA device to call down research, quotes and additional information of course, but can also start to make suggestions as they occur to the student about improvements to the lesson, the establishment, and their own business.

For example, I could be talking about utilising reflection within a business context and the student could see where such practice could impact an element of their own organisation. Normally, people think that they will take that idea back later but few actually write it down in their notes. Still fewer actually remember to take the idea they had forward when they get back to their company. Here, the idea is fresh and instantly dropped into the e-suggestion box. A DNS then automatically forwards to the proper departments or individuals who can review and assess the suggestion, with feedback or request for further information coming back live to the individual later (or even automatically routing to my knowledge bank for where the thinking came from, for example), through the same PDA.

This has two significant benefits. Firstly events occur in real time, speeding up the realisation of potential benefits (or quickly suggesting no further waste of time). For the business student, this consciously links their attendance on the training course into potential immediate benefits for their organisation. Secondly however, such interaction creates a feeling of being valued by the organisation they work for. The importance of this should not be under-estimated.

In the end, it comes down to understanding that process, system and technical changes made to improve internal working and communication mean nothing without a cultural change that has to be seen coming from, and involving, the top, that stipulates and encourages the exchange of knowledge across all aspects of said organisation.

Conversely, cultural change without the system, process and/or technical processes in place to support it will also be an ad hoc affair. Those processes don't necessarily have to be built around the concept of a digital nervous system but it seems to me that there is a natural synergy between the technical and process solution provided by a DNS implementation, and the embedding of the cultural change needed by a successful following of The Round Table Principle.

Setting up a Round Table culture will take a huge amount of initial effort, and definitely needs to be carefully planned and embedded within a formal change management programme. But the potential beneficial results of doing so would be truly incredible.

Try something else...

Go back to Focus Area 5: Play Nice and think about how you work with your work force or team.

Principle 5: The Round Table Principle in Summary.

There are several key concepts to The Round Table Principle.

1. Everyone in your organisation has some skill, experience, contact, knowledge, idea or piece of information that could be vital to the success of your organisation's success.
2. Bad news must travel fast so that your organisation can learn and improve.
3. Cultural change to embed the Principle must be supported by process and system change.
4. A focus on taking action on continuous and never-ending assessment and evaluation must be the norm.

Coping with indigestion?

Q: You've said a couple of times that band news must travel fast. Surely that leads us open to some embarrassing PR?

A: Possibly, but wouldn't it be far more economically damaging as an even greater PR disaster if the same thing happened again later? Our instinct to bury bad news means we never truly learn the lesson of why the bad thing happened in the first place. And even if you assess that a system change needs to occur to stop it occurring again, without the proper communication to your staff about why their department is suddenly facing massive disruption such an implementation could foster further issues down the line (morale, resentments etc.).

Principle 6

The Unexpected Guest Principle!
Ask the unthinkable question!

Your business or service could literally be destroyed overnight. Not because you were careless with your finances, or a competitor has manufactured a slightly cheaper widget than yours, or simply has a better workforce, but because someone not even on your radar changed the name of the game. Think Nokia and Apple iPHONE.

We all have been through the scenario! We have prepared a small, intimate gathering of close friends for an evening of fine cuisine, music and conversation. But one of the friends brings someone along that you didn't know was coming, and what's more, wouldn't have invited at all if you'd known. Welcome to the world of the unexpected guest.

Such a situation is embarrassing (and in extreme cases, distressing) enough when confined to your dinner party, imagine it happening on such a scale that your whole organisation is left rent and savaged.

Unexpected events are a nightmare to try and anticipate and plan for because, of course, they are exactly that, unexpected.

So let's give this unexpected guest a name, and we call the guest *Change*. Now we all think we know Change and what Change is. But I wonder how many of us are willing to accept what a funny thing Change can be. Change can happen so slowly we don't really notice it passing us by; or it can happen in a heartbeat. Both forms can be fatal if we're not prepared for them. So better be prepared

Let me give you an example. In chapter 2, on how we should all become our own expert, I made a quip about "anyone can make a mistake, said the Dalek climbing off the dustbin."

But as I saved it I remembered that actually nearly all dustbins today are plastic, they are no longer made of metal! Metal dustbins upside down looked like Daleks... no, honestly! The nearest quip equivalent today however, because the refuse bins are now made of plastic, would be- "Anyone can make a mistake, said the Auton climbing off the dustbin", but you'd have to be a real Dr Who fanatic to get that one. A subtle change in materials (to reduce production costs) to collect our refuse, implemented over many years, had done away with a classic one-liner.

Words of Wisdom

"It isn't that they can't see the solution. It is that they can't see the problem." GK Chesterton.

The fact is, change occurs all the time, most of it not in the least dramatic or earth shattering, but occurring nevertheless. Why then is the most prevalent reaction amongst we humans the urge to resist any change, when noticed, with all our might? I mean, after all, if not for change, we'd all still be in the ocean missing out on cars, politics, digital watches and celeb driven voyeurism. Okay, so maybe that's not such a *good* comparison, but you know what I mean.

The point is, change is good and also a natural event, so why not embrace change and in fact, even plan to take advantage of it?

Unfortunately, there's some pre-programmed response-*driven* reasons why change has such a bad reputation: "meet the new boss, same as the old boss", or, "the more things change the more they remain the same"- and most of us will have been through some agenda driven change programme at work that was cost cutting or even worse solely ego based and had nothing to do with business agility or service improvement (i.e. change for change sake). When the LibCon government was elected in 2010, many of their initial announcements about cancellation of work or changes to policy fell into this camp, having nothing to do with improving service or reducing costs, but were simply about dogma. Which is a shame, because some of the subsequent announcements *were* interesting and well thought out- they were tarred with the "dogma" brush and not therefore received properly. Don't even get me started about the Government agenda from 2015 onwards.

But for all that, change *is* good.

Let me give you an example. The internet has changed many things about the way we shop. Amazon, eBay, eBid and the likes are all good examples of how we, the public, have come to expect shopping for certain goods to be done. I use these primarily for books, gadgets, comics, DVDs and games because I use the internet mostly for shopping for these items. I sometimes buy food and wine, travel and insurance online too- it's easier, more relaxing and I don't have to leave my work environment to do it (which reminds me, why do organisations get so heated about employees doing personal online stuff in the office? If I know I can get some shopping bought online in ten minutes for delivery later, then I'm not likely to go for an hour plus at my lunchtime to get it done then, am I?). And I've been doing such shopping since before the internet was such an embedded term.

But even I was a little hesitant about getting my spectacles online when a friend suggested it. To me, getting glasses follows the traditional approach to getting service, and is not really suitable for e-shopping! Luckily, I realised that such a reaction is what did for the dodo so I thought I would try it out anyway, and I am so glad that I did.

A quick look at Martins Moneysavingexpert.com website convinced me that the one to look at was Glasses Direct (www.glassesdirect.com). Two young men set up the company in 2004 and all I can say about the glassesdirect experience is wow. The website is a joy to navigate, the process is as easy to follow as 1-2-3 and the service is unbelievable, especially when one takes into account the inexpensive charging (£400 designer glasses from £79????). It took me just 30 minutes to go to the site, have a look around, work out the offers, pick four styles I thought I liked and click 'send them to me'. This was on a Sunday afternoon. On Tuesday the 4 sets of glasses arrived for me to try out and see which really did suit me. I had easy to follow instructions of what to do next, and I ordered the very next day. Oh yes, and you could get 2 for 1. And they could be DIFFERENT styles and configurations.

Easy. Elegant. *Change*.

Change should be embraced by local government and technology adopted and adapted where appropriate- though not in the ways discussed in Principle 3: The Jewish Vampire Principle.

Change should also be planned for but implemented only when necessary. The necessary might be because of a short term problem, or a long term identification of a shift in your market, or workforce demographics or possible dramatic shifts.

It is vitally important that you take time out and plan for change and to do this you need to ask the unthinkable question posed by Joel Barker in his book Future Vision: "Ask yourself; what is totally impossible in my industry that if it was possible would totally change the rules of the game?"

It's a hard question but if you were working in California in the Vinyl industry in the late 80s, producing around 80% (if I remember correctly) of the world's supply of LP vinyl, all you were doing was watching the competitor down the road- what improvements to quality, what savings, or what new partnerships had they made etc. Along came Philips from a small country in Europe with something that was not an improvement in vinyl but a brand new technology all together- the CD. Within 2 years, your vinyl company and that of most of your "competitors" was gone.

You must plan for such events.

And you cannot allow the intransigence of 'the threatened' to block such change. For example, in Local Government, many Councillors reacted badly to the Community Call for Action legislation, and related policies such as community asset management, participatory budgeting etc. that were introduced by the Labour Government. The reaction was so bad that 'Community Call for Action' was re-branded 'Councillor Call for Action'.

The subsequent Coalition Government's plans to enhance this legislation and devolve power still further to community level, led to renewed resistance from the Councillors. The reaction of many elected members in a recent online conference discussing the use of social media to interlock services directly with the public was of the "yes it's great but only if conducted through us Councillors; officers should be barred from talking to my voters!" In other words, these members fear that direct access to officers would remove the need for members of the public to seek *their* help. After all, if you can chat one evening via Facebook to your local environment officer, why would you need to pop round to see the Councillor and express your views on Number 49's front garden so he/she can thump a desk on your behalf?

However, the biggest thing to understand about change is that when you come to make changes, you have to take your organisation with you. Don't assume that all your staff understand why you're making changes, or will accept them gracefully even if they do understand the reasons why. Above all, don't be like a certain Local Government HR Director I know who thinks her role is about suppressing that 'not to be trusted workforce' who can't be trusted to be involved in any necessary restructure so she'd better just threaten them all with the sack if they don't sign up to the third fait accompli in 2 years. This is NOT effective change management.

Change, however, is fantastic when done correctly and for the right reasons. It can even create brand new opportunities for your business and/or service.

Take a bite...

Call a meeting with key decision makers and known thinkers and ideas personnel and ask the question: "What event or development might occur in the future that, however unlikely it might be, devastate our business/service delivery? Frame the question with the following statement: NOTHING IS TO BE CONSIDERED TOO OFF THE WALL.

Brainstorm every possible situation and then review them one by one by first doing a simple SWOT analysis and then come up with possible strategies to deal with it should the situation, no matter how unlikely, occur.

An example of an industry that should definitely be looking to the future and coming up with strategies accordingly is the airline industry. Around the year 2000 I gave a presentation to influential members of the industry about what was happening with IT and the plans of the major manufacturers, and the possible impact such plans might have on their market in the future.

As a bit of fun I included a 5 minute look at what IBM were doing with developments in teleportation theory and technology, concluding with a real magazine advert that IBM had run in certain highly technical magazines promoting a desktop teleporter[63], a device that IBM felt they could have in production in some 50 years.

The bit of fun turned into a very heated debate, with the table of air industry leaders splitting down the middle between those who dismissed it as science fiction[64] and those who were clearly shaken by one simple fact: 33% of the airline industry's revenues come from freight. IBM could wipe out that revenue literally overnight if they succeeded in developing devices that could teleport non-organic materials at the push of a computer return key.

My recommendations were for the airline industry to fund quantum entanglement research teams and patent technologies and applications arising from their work- and maybe even team up with IBM to develop specific airport distribution solutions.

At this time, it seems that the doubters won the day and no such investment programme has, as far as I know, been implemented. The opportunity lost here is even more striking given that at the time of the original presentations, the airline industry was incredibly cash rich. In these days of post-911 and rising fuel prices, such speculative investments are now regarded as a luxury that they cannot afford to make.

I would argue that they cannot afford *not* to.

For example, when Ford produced his first trucks in 1923, one of the world's largest rail companies (and one of the USA's biggest companies) had an opportunity to purchase the lot. They turned down the opportunity because they were, in their estimation, in the rail industry. They were in fact in the *transportation* industry and saw their freight

---

[63] For more information on teleportation see my new book "The 50 Year Horizon: Science & Technology for Non-believers."- out soon.

[64] It isn't, the technology is based on real scientific principles and observed experiments around what is called quantum entanglement.

revenues cut by two thirds within a decade. The company itself no longer exists, having gone out of business in the early 1980s after decades of decline.

Atari and Commodore were in the top 5 PC companies in the world in the 1970s and 1980s. But they were their own competitors and ignored the growing economies of scale within the WINTEL manufacturing base that led to huge price drops and technological advances. By the time of the 486, Atari and Commodore were out of the business and education worlds and were dropping market share in their core consumer market at such a rate that they were out of business within another technological refresh from Intel.

Today, traditional phone companies such as NOKIA have been knocked down and are facing the final count, not because Motorola or Ericson came up with a better phone, but because two companies not even in the phone marketplace 5 years ago, Apple and Blackberry, made mobile phones into a completely new media and communications platform. However as technology and markets change at an ever increasing rate, Blackberry is already struggling to adapt, and even Apple's iPhone sales have started to stall.

So, what tech-quake could happen to your industry? Who could come knocking at your door with a brand new way of doing something that makes your delivery service a thing of the past?

If you aren't asking these questions on a regular basis and making serious plans to mitigate against the answers, then you risk becoming a vinyl record manufacturer, or an Atari, or a Nokia. So plan for the Unexpected Guest before he comes knocking. You have been warned.

Try something else...

The Unexpected Guest Principle can be powerfully combined with Principle 12: The 99 Monkeys Principle.

More Words of Wisdom?

"There are known knowns. These are things we know that we know. There are known unknowns. That is to say, there are things that we know we don't know. But there are also unknown unknowns. There are things we don't know we don't know." Donald Rumsfeld

Principle 6: The Unexpected Guest Principle in Summary.

You must ask, and answer, on a regular basis (at least once a year but more if possible) the following question: What event or development, no matter how unlikely, should it occur, cause massive problems for my organisation?

Coping with indigestion?

Q: How off the wall should we go before things become silly?

A: *Obviously, there comes a point when you have to make judgement calls about some of the ideas or suggestions. The trick is not to dismiss ANYTHING out of hand to start with. The format of your Unexpected Guest workshop should be to first capture any and all suggestions about events or developments, no matter how impossible they may at first appear to be. Only start to evaluate them once this process has been exhausted.*

Q: Surely we can't plan for everything though?

A: *Of course you can't. It's impossible to anticipate absolutely everything that could occur at some unspecified point in the future. But if you visit this scenario once a year with your best thinkers- and because they know it's every year they will prepare for the meeting by reading and following a wider library of opinions- then you start to create plans and strategies that form a knowledge bank of tools that could be readily adapted to suit other issues should they occur.*

Note too that whilst I said have the TUG Workshop annually, for the first year I would do them quarterly to create the momentum and culture change needed to start to think beyond what is happening right now.

Principle 7

The Chameleon Principle!

Adapt or die! Yes, it really is that simple.

Life is going fast these days. Changes in your market place occur at an ever increasing rate. Our knowledge of life, the universe and everything doubles every 5 years! So, doing what you've always done isn't really a good idea is it?

Albert Einstein said: "The significant problems we face cannot be solved at the same level of thinking we were at when we created them."[65]

How many times have you experienced the following situations?

- You've started work in a new position and whilst doing your normal duties, you notice that an internal process your department is using could be speeded up by removing a layer of sign off. When you point it out you're told that the process was implemented by the current MD when the business was just starting out so that he could keep tight control of budgets and is unlikely to be changed.

---

[65] For more on Einstein's thinking that can be applied directly to business processes, see The Einstein Principle (Principle 9).

- You work on the board of a company that has been the dominant market leader for over a generation, but recently your market share has been declining and the profit per sale has halved. When you mention your concerns at the board meeting, the other board members seem not to be concerned about it because such market cycles have happened before and the company has always regained a commanding market share.
- You have come from a new company that has a better and more efficient system in place for processing orders, but when you speak to the office manager she says that this is the process they have always used and she doesn't see any need to change it now.

All the responses and thinking habits that I just described are exactly the responses and thinking habits that meant within three years of the publication of "In Search of Excellence: Lessons from America's best run companies."[66], fully one quarter of the companies featured within it were in trouble.

Think about that. These were the companies portrayed as the best of the best and had steadily, over decades in some cases, built up a strong, stable and in most cases a dominant market position, and yet literally within 36 months, they were ailing companies suffering incredible losses and tough times. Why?

Well, you could of course blame the economic downturn in the mid 80s, but the reality is that these companies simply didn't adapt to the changes going on around them. They didn't keep pace with the level of change, or notice new threats arising from companies that were not even in their primary markets when the book had been written. In effect, they kept to the same level of thinking, used the same strategies and processes, and behaved in the same way that had made them a success in the first place. And they were punished for their complacency.

---

[66] Published in 1982 and written by Tom Peters and Robert H Waterman.

Words of Wisdom

"It is not necessary to change. Survival is not mandatory." W. Edwards Deming

The Chameleon Principle then is all about adapting to your surroundings and creating for yourself the best possible scenario for success. Chameleons of course are a distinctive and highly specialised lizard. They are distinguished by parrot-like zygodactylism feet, separately mobile and stereoscopic eyes, their very long, highly modified and rapid darting tongues, swaying gait, the possession by many of a prehensile tail, crests or horns on their distinctively shaped heads, and the ability of some to change colour.

The many evolutionary adaptations that chameleons possess all add to their ability to survive in some pretty hostile environments and so adopting similar abilities must be a priority for any organisation that wishes to have continued existence. Other Principles in this book are eminently geared towards being used in tandem with this Principle, especially The Unexpected Guest Principle (TUG) which obviously focuses the mind on what changes could occur that may mean you need to make massive adaptations in your business structure or model.

Adaptations in your organisation should almost always be gradual, incremental improvements in the processes, service or product offerings and systems that you run, avoiding any massive revolutionary advancements unless your TUG workshop identifies a potential threat or opportunity that would necessitate such a change occurring. On these occasions, you should of course manage the massive upheaval with massive consideration for your staff, suppliers and your clients.

The beauty of having the TUG Principle in place and the creation of a change culture within your organisation from the start means that you should rarely have to adapt because you are reacting to a body blow that caught you completely by surprise.

Take a bite...

Set up a ThinkTank Group with the responsibility of doing a baseline analysis of all your systems, processes, products/services and the market environment in which you operate. They should make suggestions for incremental improvements in the baselines and feed directly into the TUG Workshops and Board meetings on a regular basis. This group should also take direction from the TUG Workshops about what areas to look at.

If you're a new business or entrepreneur, set up a focus group with close friends or family members who have relevant skills, a trusted client and/or supplier and anyone else you think might be able to help.

There's not a lot more to say about this Principle because it is so patently simple and practical to implement- except that it is precisely because it is so simple that you must think about the implications of a proper implementation of it. Lip service is not sufficient enough, nor is simply knowing the concept behind it. The idea that every part of your organisation continually improves its systems and reviews its purpose, direction and focus must be embedded as a normal part of the daily routine.

The Japanese know this and call it Kaizen. Tony Robbins calls it CANI (constant and never-ending improvement). Whatever you call it you must implement it. Peter Drucker said that, "Significant competitive advantage lies with those organisations and individuals who anticipate well in turbulent times." That sounds like good thinking to me. I shall also leave you with this last, related thought: in business, a good manager is someone who can solve problems as they occur. A leader is someone who anticipates potential problems in advance and deals with them before they occur. Which are you?

Try something else...

The Chameleon Principle can be powerfully combined with Principle 6: The Unexpected Guest Principle.

Principle 7: The Chameleon Principle in Summary.

You must embed within your organisation a focus on constant but, wherever possible, incremental improvements or adaptations to every single aspect of your organisation.

Coping with indigestion?

Q: Isn't all this improvement all the time going to cost a lot of money?

A: It shouldn't because we're talking about incremental changes to your systems and processes, and in fact some of these improvements can save you money, e.g. reducing a layer of bureaucracy in an ordering system, or delegating decision making powers to reduce bottlenecks.

If you're talking about spends on equipment (e.g. software solutions as an example) you should be budgeting for annual reviews and improvements anyway (although I am NOT advocating that you upgrade your Oracle database every year!).

The question you should really be asking is can we afford to have a major change forced upon us should the conditions in our marketplace abruptly alter?

Principle 8

The Prometheus Principle!

Be a god. Bring the gift of fire!

You have your vision. You have your goals and objectives. You have a mission statement. And you have a marketing plan. But do any of these fail to excite you? Do any of them fail to support the others? If you answered yes then you need to rip them up and start again.

Words have power! It's that oft spoken cliché that the pen is indeed mightier than the sword. Yes, words have power, but what about the person speaking them? How fired up are you?

In Greek mythology, Prometheus is a Titan, the son of Iapetus and Themis, and brother to Atlas, Epimetheus and Menoetius. He was a champion of mankind, known for his wily intelligence, and acting in this role stole fire from Zeus and gave it to mortals. Zeus subsequently punished him for his crime by having him bound to a rock while a great eagle ate his liver only to have it grow back to be eaten again the next day. His myth has been treated by a number of ancient sources, in which Prometheus is credited with playing a pivotal role in the early history of mankind. During the Greek War of Independence, Prometheus even became a figure of hope and inspiration for Greek revolutionaries and their philhellene supporters.

It is in this idea of the gift of fire that I wish to focus on here. I've already spoken about the need to create your vision and express your goals in plain English but using emotive language. The reason for this, as I gave in earlier chapters, is that if we use language that excites and motivates us to act, then we automatically generate heat and energy because *we* are excited and motivated. Setting out a vision that says we will have the best widgets and become market leaders won't excite you as much as a vision that says our widgets will be the lynchpin used in world changing technologies!

The Prometheus Principle therefore incorporates two focal points:

1. The Self. In other words, what do you need to do to bring fire to your own day to day routines and to that of your organisation as a whole?
2. The Message. This means all your printed materials, e-media usage, media broadcasts AND your plans, including your Marketing & PR Plan.

Now, I know there are some executives and managers out there shaking their heads at the moment: emotion should be kept out of business, a precept that they have lived and breathed for their entire career. But it is a wrong precept. As an executive you may well enjoy getting up every morning, driving (or being driven) in your Lexus or Jaguar to the office and getting stuck in to the day to day routine of decision making, lunches, meetings, corridors of power excursions and having your ego stroked by your PA (who actually does most of the actual work) - and all the trappings and pay and bonuses and share options that go with it are all the motivation you need.

But what about everyone else? What about the receptionist who gets paid in a year what you make in a month or day, who has to deal with often rude visitors or callers and pushy sales people and then take the 90 minute bus and train ride home in grotty weather and dirty vehicles? What can help motivate him or her? Your mission statement dictated from upon high that says what you think it should say but which has no relation to the day to day operations of your business? I don't think so.

Words of Wisdom

"Seeing into darkness is clarity" Lao Tzu

Language can be incredibly moving and change the entire mood of a nation. Don't believe me? How about these examples then?

- *Ask not what your country can do for you, rather, what can you do for your country?*
- *I have a dream.*
- *We shall fight them on the beaches…*

Now, if words can galvanise a country into changing its course and adopting a new sense of purpose, imagine what they could do to something much smaller, such as your company or organisation! Or even you!

As a reminder therefore, you must get everyone involved in the creation of your company vision and/or mission statement so that all employees feel a sense of belonging to your organisation that goes well beyond that of the pay-cheque club. The final version should be in plain English but use emotive language that instils a positive feeling within you and your staff.

You must, daily, live and breathe and act in a way that is consistent with that vision. If your company vision is to change the world, losing your temper at the young intern who has mislaid a report is hardly in keeping with that vision. You must therefore embed the power of *your* vision within *your* psyche, remind yourself at every opportunity what it is and what it means and lead by example. You, in effect, must be Prometheus to the mortals.

Now, all this may sound like typical guru hyperbole but I am being totally serious- you must lead by example. If you live and breathe with a passion for what you are doing, it shows up in everything that you do, and people working for you will subliminally pick up on your constant behaviour and respond accordingly. The same is true if you behave in an uncaring or aggressive way. The culture of *any* organisation will reflect the culture of the people at the top. Even multi-national corporations. The effect on small organisations is even more dramatic and immediate.

Sadly, all too often I have seen people at executive levels behave with an arrogant disregard for the rank & file, and sometimes with an almost divide-and-conquer mentality. In the short run such a board (or individual manager) exerts massive control and rules by fear. IN the longer term however, such an approach creates massive problems with confrontational activity, subversion and a complete lack of loyalty that spreads into your suppliers and clients.

Here's the process. The Board bully the senior management team (SMT) to get results. The SMT bully their team leaders to get results. The team leaders bully their staff to get results. The staff complain to one another and then moan to clients that they have built up personal relationships with. End result: a company that NO-ONE feels any loyalty toward.

So control your own nature and be a god. After all, wouldn't you prefer your employees to be in awe of you rather than demonise you?

The second area of focus for The Prometheus Principle is on your message. Check all your text- adverts, presentation scripts, email templates, social media posts, leaflets, company reports, brochures, adverts, business cards, mission statement, marketing plan etc- and make sure that ALL the following statements are true:

1. The message is clear.
2. The words are in plain English.
3. The words are expressed with passion and commitment.
4. There is a call for action.

Take a bite...

Pick just one marketing material and your mission statement or business tagline and, along with your Marketing & PR department, analyse it in detail against the 4 statements on page 208. Make it clear to your team that you want them to take apart all other materials with the same focus and replace them as soon as possible with the new words. Email templates and web messages should of course be altered within the week.

The important thing to recognise here is that such a change in focus won't only benefit your organisation. By embracing passion and a positive belief in your products or services, and then acting daily in accordance with that passion and belief, you own character and general mood will improve as well. Your view on life generally will change and what might start out as a conscious effort will simply become who you are.

The reason for this is that our brain does not want to make us a liar. That's why we are always able to justify actions that are not in our best interest. Know smoking is bad for you but can't stop? You probably have rationalised that you pick up good intelligence from the smokers corner, or that you could get hit by a bus tomorrow anyhow, so why worry? Love your partner but have a one night stand? You were caught in a moment of weakness or had too much to drink!

So if you need to fool your brain in adopting a new rationalised identity, why not make it a positive one? And it starts by creating the words you need to have that dialogue.

Try something else...

The Prometheus Principle obviously links directly with Focus Area 3: Create your vision.

Principle 8: The Prometheus Principle in Summary.

You cannot create passion in your employees or from your clients unless you yourself act in a passionate and inspiring way day to day. Your internal passion must then be represented in all your external marketing materials.

Coping with indigestion?

Q: Are you saying we should lie to ourselves and staff by acting passionately about our widgets even if we can't see any reason to do so?

A: No, I am saying you must find an aspect of what you do that gives you the passion to behave in an inspirational way on a constant and consistent basis. You must then change all your marketing efforts to reflect that passion. If you TRULY can't then you need to find a job that can create that internal fire.

Q: Is it wise to bring emotion into business?

A: If you are confusing passion with aggression or anger then no, it's not wise. Yet of all the emotions in business I have encountered over the decades it's those negatives ones that show up time and again. And it is those same angry managers who will reject the need for passionate belief, happy & joyful persona and positive can do attitudes as "hippy hug a tree stuff." Bizarre.

Principle 9

The Einstein Principle!

The art of developing ESP[67] is within reach!

Many people think that Einstein was just a simple scientist who went about formulating the laws that govern the Universe, but he was *so* much more than that.

Apart from being the man who had the greatest single impact on the advancement of our understanding of the laws that govern the physical universe, Einstein was also a philosopher king! Following are some of his musings, along with how they can relate to your business.

For this chapter we're going to change the format somewhat. As we've said old Albert was a wise old coot whose musings have a wider impact on the world than just the scientific achievements you're probably more familiar with. We call these musings ESPs, or Einstein Sub-Principles. Each ESP is an Einstein saying that has a direct correlation to how

---

[67] Einstein Sub-Principles

organisations and businesses are designed and run. So we'll print the saying and then apply the logic. There are several of these, and all of the ESPs combined make The Einstein Principle. As such there are no 'words of wisdom' sections as the whole chapter is about words of wisdom, or a Take a Bite section as suggestions are made within each ESP.

Clear?

It isn't? Well, okay, read on and hopefully you'll get the gist of what I mean as we go along.

ESP1:   "The search for truth is more precious than its possession."

This of course links back into the idea that you should never stop learning, and asking questions so that you *can* learn. It is Stephen Covey's "sharpening the saw" principle, and underpins many of the concepts and principles to be found within this book, especially The Maverick, Round Table, Confucius & Chameleon Principles (see how this book is starting to hang together?). The journey (search) becomes the thing, rather than just the destination. In other words if you can create a culture where your employees are always looking to improve, discover and push forward their processes, systems & their own individual skills, then your company will grow at a far more rapid rate than those organisations that simply accept the status quo.

In a business & public service context of course this can also relate to the drive to tick boxes rather than to create sustainable programmes. It is the realisation that we've hit the target but missed the point. A practical application would be to create a rewards system based on contribution rather than simply bottom line revenue earning or how many tick box style outputs have been achieved. Rewarding someone for simply doing their job constantly at an excellent rate rather than just achieving all the objectives set out in the PDR will generate more heat *and* light. It will instil within them a more definite sense of belonging to the company and that can never be a bad thing.

ESP 2: "Imagination is more important than knowledge."

In my Far Horizons lectures I always end with a slide that plays the Star Trek overture (original series) which shows a starship swinging away from a planet before bursting into Warp drive just as the "dur- de- dur, dur dur de dur, de pa pa pap PARRRR" reaches a crescendo, with the words above and then Albert Einstein appearing as the trumpet sound fades.

This ESP is one of those ideas that has no direct application, but is such a powerful belief to install within your psyche, it can influence everything you do. It starts with the idea that "there is no such thing as a stupid question" and ends with the concept of understanding that thinking outside the box is not as effective as realising *there is no box to begin with*. In other words, don't approach a problem from the point of view it can't be solved, or that is going to bankrupt you trying to solve it. Instead rebalance the Unexpected Guest question into: If there were no limits, what could I do to destroy this problem? Brainstorm everything out, don't evaluate until you can't think of any other ideas. You'll find an answer, trust me.

ESP 3: "No amount of experimentation can ever prove me right; a single experiment can prove me wrong."

In science, nothing is ever 100% true. Think about that axiom. True science merely posits a theorem that should it be successful tested and validated by other independent scientists, raises up a ranking to being a theory. When further tests validate the theory still further, the theory does not become an automatic truth. It remains a theory until the next set of tests can be devised to see if the theory still meets with observable predictions.

One experiment that shows unpredicted observations (usually the opposite of what is expected) can destroy the theory overnight.

This relates to the idea of leadership. A leader is often only ever as good as his or her last successful decision. But the truth is, even the best business mind will get it wrong. Virgin Coke? ZapMail? PS/1? The world is full of wrong decisions made by very successful people and organisations. The trick is not falling into the trap of defining a wrong decision as a BAD decision.

In effect, this ESP could be said to be a combination of flexing the decision making muscle, and also being a chameleon and adapting to your surroundings. A leader is someone who, after listening to advice for a LIMITED amount of time, makes a decision and takes action. The Latin root of decide means "to cut off from", in other words, once a course of action is decided upon, the leader does not flip back and forth when obstacles and problems arise.

Successful leaders however, are those who realise that deciding on a course of action is not the same as never adapting the approach. There are many ways to get to the same destination- just ask a light photon![68] You must be aware of what is happening around you and change your approach accordingly. Planes do not fly across the Atlantic in a perfectly straight line. If they did they wouldn't need pilots. It is the pilot's job to make constant micro changes in the course the plane is flying to account for winds, atmospheric conditions, even sunspots.

You must do the same. Make your decisions quickly, but allow the methods of achieving the outcomes to vary.

ESP 4: "Most people say that is it is the intellect which makes a great scientist. They are wrong: it is character."

Apart from having a brain the size of a planet, Einstein was a man of constant inquisition, determination and almost child-like playfulness. It was these traits that turned him around from being a student of

---

[68] If this joke is over your head, don't worry, buy my new book "The 50 Year Horizon: Science & Technology for Non-believers." out soon or attend one of my science talks.

average achievement into the man who changed forever our understanding of the universe and the forces at play within it.

And in case you're one of the people who just take relativity and the speed of light for granted, he did all this at a time when many scientists still believed that light travelled across an almost mystical ether and therefore the voids of space were not true vacuums, but full of this *stuff*. Think about it. His achievements were huge.

It is the same with anyone who sets themselves up as a leader, even (or especially) in a business context. I have seen managers who have all the paper qualifications under the sun but are still terrible managers and even worse leaders. They simply did not have the patience, empathy or humour to manage people effectively, or the imagination and vision to be a leader.

So whilst you are getting your business qualifications do so without sacrificing your social and thinking skills. If you are lacking in some areas, then go outside your comfort zone and learn how to gain those skills.

ESP 5: "It's not that I'm so smart, it's just that I stay with problems longer."

Einstein was an amazingly humble man, but this typical self-effacing statement reveals much of the secret of his success. He simply refused to give up. In everything he did, Einstein took the approach of an outstanding man who wanted to achieve outstanding things.

Tony Robbins talks about being outstanding in these terms. Imagine you start off in a job. If you're bad at it, what's your reward? You get fired! That's the floor.

But let's imagine you do a good job. What are the rewards you get? *POOR* rewards. That's right, not good rewards, but *poor*. Say that's about the height of your waist.

Some people however aren't content with being good, they strive for excellence! And they achieve it and get…. good rewards! It doesn't seem right does it, there you are pumping out excellence all over the place and you're left with the question: *is this it? Is this all I get?* And it's about here, at the level of your scalp, where many people give up. After all, what's the point? They work so hard, push to be completely excellent at everything they do, and only end up with a *good* life style.

This is a shame, because the Aladdin's cave of treasures comes to those who are consistently outstanding. The leap from good reward to treasure trove reward is huge! But if we've said the leap from bad to good effort is a huge one, and the leap from good to excellent is an even larger leap- and for disappointedly corresponding rewards, then the leap from excellent to outstanding must be at the height of the ceiling, right?

Wrong. The leap from being excellent to becoming outstanding is literally an inch above your head. It is the smallest shift in what you do and how you act and behave, and yet brings with it the greatest shift in rewards.

So ask yourself, when have you almost had everything in the palm of your hands but at the last moment, failed to make that extra little tiptoe effort (for whatever reason) and seen the treasure fall out of sight?

I bet there are several instances. I know I've been guilty of it.

So be like Albert, stay at it longer. Push *that* little bit harder. I'm not saying ignore the kids, but I am saying there is nothing wrong with occasionally postponing something to get the job done.

ESP 6: "You have to learn the rules of the game. And then you have to play better than anyone else."

If you want to become a success you have to first get into the game, and to do that you have to understand what the rules are. Once you've got that locked down, you have to practice and compete constantly (sharpening the saw again) - and if necessary, push for a change in the rules!!!

One of my downfalls is a constant inability to play the politics game. Time and again I would hit barriers erected by those who felt threatened by my ideas and ability to cut through the bull and get the job done. You see, I would strive to understand better than anyone else the technology, or the service, or the market, of the process delivery model, and work hard to get the job done- but wouldn't put anytime into making sure I read the small print about what the other players might be doing in the meantime.

In the end however, I have come to a conclusion that whilst I have now developed strong diplomatic skills (sometimes I choose *not* to employ them however), I cannot be a political animal. It goes so strongly against my view of right and wrong I refuse to stroke egos or brown nose for the sake of a promotion, I decided to change the rules of the game. I set up my own business.

Now, the above statement is MY view and character and I am not saying that it is right and your view, should it differ, be wrong. It is right for me. You must choose a game that is right for you. Just play it full out.

ESP 7: "Anyone who has never made a mistake has never tried anything new."

As I have already admitted throughout this book, I have made (and continue to make) mistakes, ranging from minor inconveniences to absolute *oh my lord pass me a gun now*! But I never stop trying because I have a very simple philosophy: I never fail, so long as I learn something new (even, as I said, if that something new is- *I won't ever do that again*!).

And this is the problem with business today. We're so hung up on a management structure that punishes people when they get things wrong that no-one does anything. We are too paralysed. I live by the idea that I want my people to know that if they make 10 decisions, and get 2 wrong, they still made 8 decisions that moved things on. In fact, even the 2 wrong decisions, so long as they are quick to acknowledge and come up with corrections (or ask for help) have still moved things along because now we know 2 more things NOT to do.

Thomas Edison, creator of the light bulb, tried over 10000 times before he succeeded. On attempt 9999 (or thereabouts) he succeeded in blowing up his office, scaring the life out of his biographer and singeing off his eyebrows. When the biographer challenged Edison that maybe it was time to stop, Edison refused to acknowledge defeat. In exasperation the biographer said back words to the effect of: "You're crazy! You're never going to succeed with this, you've just failed for the 10000th time!" To which Edison replied, "I didn't fail. I learned 9999 ways of how not to create an electric light. And on this occasion I even came up with an explosive that might interest the army."

Interesting point of view, don't you think?

ESP 8: "To stimulate creativity one must develop childlike inclination for play and the childlike desire for recognition."

One of the main compliments I receive (as well as, it has to be said, the most vehement criticism) is that I am so young in my approach to life and work. I enthuse a childlike enjoyment about so many things, and, I am told, naïve positivism about what I am doing or trying to do in my business.

My outlook on life is simple: life is a journey and I want to experience everything I can before I get to the final destination. So yes, if I find it really exciting to look upon the craters of the moon with a small telescope, or catch a stunning view of sunlight breaking through a misty morning tree branch system, or get giddy when a top executive suddenly gets what I am talking about, or (best yet) seeing a previously disinterested young mind switch on to how exciting science really is, then you can call me childlike and naïve all you like.

Because I would rather happily achieve than achieve to be happy.

ESP 9: "Great ideas often receive violent opposition from mediocre minds."

It is said that any new idea must go through three stages of development.

First it is met with derision.

Then it is confronted with hostility and aggression.

Finally, it is accepted as plainly self-evident.

This is especially true when your great idea is a challenge to the established way of doing things, or contrary to the idea of the one who sits above you. I cannot tell you how often I have come up with new ways of doing something, only for it to be aggressively rejected, but then for it to implemented quietly a little after I have moved on- I gave some specific examples without mentioning names earlier in the book (take me to the pub and maybe I'll tell you the names of the culprits over a drink). To which I think, just imagine what benefits you could have already enjoyed if you had implemented the idea sooner.

Even Einstein fell into this trap when he first rejected the utter randomness of reality that arises out of quantum mechanics out of hand with the classic line: "God does not play dice with the universe." Thankfully, being a smart cookie, he later reassessed quantum physics and accepted it as being a truth that warranted further experiment.

So the next time that intern comes to you, fresh from college, with an idea of how to do something don't dismiss it out of hand. Look at it with an open mind, who knows, he or she may just have saved you a small fortune!

Try something else...

The Einstein Sub-Principles underpin so many of the Focus Areas and Principles that it is difficult to direct you to just one. Therefore check out the following:

The Confucius Principle
The Maverick Principle
The Unexpected Guest Principle
And
Flex That Decision Making Muscle

Principle 9: The Einstein Principle in Summary.

Think. Think again. And then think some more. Be imaginative, be playful, be determined, but never stop thinking.

Principle 10

The Confucius Principle!
Never stop learning!

Education has gathered some negative connotations over the years, and badly thought out and delivered training courses have extended those negative associations into adult life. But the key to advancement is continuous learning.

Even if we haven't heard the life story of Confucius we almost certainly have heard about him, and we most likely know he was a wise man.

A little while ago, I was working on promoting the Cafe Scientifique[69] motif and our own Far Horizons concept[70] to a local council and members of the public in a town that shall remain nameless. Many people, with an open mind, were really excited by what the program could mean to local aspirations and to engaging with local young people in particular. What surprised me however was the vehemently negative

---

[69] Cafe Scientifique is a place where, for the price of a cup of coffee or a glass of wine, anyone can come to explore the latest ideas in science and technology. Meetings take place in cafes, bars, restaurants and even theatres, but always outside a traditional academic context. See cafescientifique.org for details.

[70] See www.darreninform.com and my new book "The 50 Year Horizon: Science & Technology for the Non-believer."

reaction of some of the local councillors and representatives of some community groups.

Certain Councillors demanded to know where the idea had come from and why they were discussing it when it hadn't come from one of their numerous committee meetings (i.e., it wasn't their idea so why was it being given council time!); and some community activists started to spread the story that I was recruiting young people to join a new UK cult of scientologists. These rumours were then reportedly repeated by some of the Councillors. Now, all the literature and all my engagement with bodies quite clearly stated that the intention behind the program was to a) get people interested in learning and b) get young people interested in science so they could take up the highly paid roles in a regional agency funded science cluster- either as managers, researchers or indeed, scientists. These roles are not currently occupied by local people.

Now, whilst I can understand why some uneducated people might confuse scientists with scientologists (well, actually, I find it difficult to even comprehend this level of confusion, but for the sake of this chapter I shall try) I cannot understand, nor forgive, people in positions of power and influence showing such ignorance- or at least not checking the facts first. It brings a whole new meaning to the phrase "closing the skills gap" doesn't it? Scientist is to Scientologist as a bike is to a fish. There is no relationship.

Words of Wisdom

"Second only to freedom, learning is the most precious option on earth." Norman Cousins

Furthermore, such ignorance, or deliberate muddying of the waters, would make any programme for change almost impossible to undertake, wouldn't it?

Well, only if such stupidity or intransigence is left unchecked. Such ignorance MUST be challenged and shot down at every encounter and every member of the public, every elected servant, every manager, every worker and every public officer must be allowed to do so without fear of reprisal, punishment or censure. That's part of the reason why I set up The Inform Group, and in particular the ThinkWORKS service. I fully intend to challenge every bad idea, incredibly poor practice and politically/ego driven programme that makes no sense other than to promote a selfish agenda.

The fact is that one of Britain's best hopes of building a secure future for the next generation is to build on scientific programs- and to do that we must encourage them to want to learn, and learn the sciences in particular. The Independent in its 18th August 2011 edition published an article - "What Britain Needs Now Is the Appliance of Science" by Sarah Arnott, pushing exactly this belief. Science is where the money is. Science is where the growth is. And yet, we do not promote science to our young people in a way to get them interested, or excited. In short, we do not make science sexy.

This isn't true everywhere of course. A small village school, initially under the leadership of the then head teacher and the departmental head of science, decided to make the school everything about science. Its success, in particular in engaging with its pupils, was astounding. It became the first science college in the borough, its young people and, crucially, their families, became involved in many projects connected to the environment and other science projects (including support for Bloodhound, the UK project to design and build the world's fastest car), its results improved dramatically and it is still the only village Cafe Sci in the world. I am, of course, proud to say that I also played a small role in this development but it was the vision of the staff that was the driver- and they had a manager (the head teacher) who not only allowed the vision to thrive, but actively supported it.

This is what is needed more than ever: the active support of management when employees or customers come up with new ideas and ways of doing things. And none of us should allow blind ignorance and selfish interest to stop it.

Now, I don't want to turn this book into a political tract but I mention the above to illustrate an important point: *it is through the application of knowledge that dramatic changes occur*. And that knowledge is gathered through the act of *learning*.

Take a bite...

Tonight, when you get home, sit with a cup of tea or glass of wine and on a piece of paper write down all the things you've learned today that you didn't know before. No, I don't mean the latest squeeze that Karen from admin is hooked up with. I mean something new about the world, your business, a customer thinking process, or a fact in general. If you can't think of anything, go get that encyclopaedia of the shelf, blow the dust off and pick a page at random.

Do this for 30 days. Cultivate the habit.

We've already said that one of the main areas cut by companies in hard times is their training programme, yet to me this makes no sense. The best asset you have is your people, *always*. But *only* if they are utilised correctly. And to get the best out of them they have to be both at their best *and* know that they are appreciated for it.

Sending your staff therefore on a training course to improve their management abilities, or IT capabilities, is not an unaffordable luxury, it is an essential necessity! Only by doing this do you continue to build a competitive edge over your nearest rivals, and not simply because you have improved the skills of your employee but also because you have made that employee feel valued and supported.

Now, the issue is that so many so called management courses are poor and don't bring anything worthwhile back to your organisation, so one thing you must take responsibility for is checking out courses yourself. I am not saying that you should book yourself on all of them of course, simply that you must research them (or if you have an HR department, make sure that someone there has properly researched both the course *and* the company delivering it).

One other thing to think about too is when an employee comes to you with a wish to do a course that, on the face of it, doesn't seem to have much to do with their day job. You'll be surprised sometimes how such a course can still benefit your organisation simply because it rounds off the employee in such a way that they are able to function better at work.

Try something else...

If you're turned on by learning and improving your knowledge and skills every day, take a look at Focus Area 2: Become Your Own Expert.

In conclusion then this principle is a simple, but foundational concept that should underpin your daily approach to work and, God forbid, your life. If every day you go into that day with the approach that says *I will consciously note every single new idea, fact or piece of information I receive this day,* pretty soon you build up an impressive bank of knowledge and new skills.

Furthermore, after a while such an approach becomes a habit; in effect you programme your brain to notice such things automatically.

The trick is then to make sure you start to apply what you learn; only then do you start to become a wise man/woman.

Principle 10: The Confucius Principle in Summary.

Become wise by consciously learning something new every day, and then applying what you've learned where it is applicable.

Coping with indigestion?

Q: Ok, I think I get what you're saying about the importance of education and training, but are you really saying I should send Janet from admin on to a part time PGCE course?

A: *Why not? Obviously you have to know her reasons and what she intends to do with it, but if one of those reasons is because she wants to start training new members of staff in how to use the internal systems and processes, then this could increase the efficiency of your admin support, reduce costly mistakes and speed up order processing. The trick is not to just dismiss any request for training until you have; a) heard their reasons and justifications for wanting to do it, and; b) properly assessed the potential benefits to your business.*

Q: But I've paid for people to do training courses and even Diplomas in Management Studies and then they've simply left the organisation. Why should I pay for someone else to get the benefits?

A: *If you are paying for someone to do a course there is nothing wrong with putting in place a contract that says should the person leave within a year of completion (except on grounds of ill-health or catastrophic family reasons of course), that they should repay the fees within a certain period of time. You should also encourage the employee to start to apply what they are learning immediately. In other words, don't just passively agree to a training course, make sure you have an agreed plan to follow up.*

Principle 11

The Gaia Principle!
Everything is connected to everything else!

James Lovelock, former astronaut and not someone psychologically given to flights of fancy, has proposed a simple and elegant idea: we should think of the world as a living, breathing entity and every creature and process of nature is part of that entity's bio-system. You should think the same way about your business.

Remember that old song (Dem Bones); "the toe bone is connected to the foot bone, the foot bone is connected to the ankle bone, the ankle bone is connected to..." and so on? Your business is like that. Completely interconnected to everything else.

My company, The Inform Group, was originally set up to help small businesses, 3rd sector and community groups start up, grow or undergo change management. We worked on the principle that getting people into learning, self-employment or work is for the good of everyone, which is why the sound bites put forward by the coalition government in 2010 regarding helping people back into employment or, even better, to set up their own business to generate new employment opportunities, resounded loudly to us.

Unfortunately, the pronouncements became nothing more *than* sound bites. Even worse, the programme of cut announcements moved in exactly the opposite direction from the stated intention.

As said previously, I have no wish to turn this book into a political discourse and I suspect I would be writing these words regardless of the political colour of our government. The point I am trying to make here is that everything really *is* connected to everything else.

Let's take a further look then at the stated belief that the nation will be saved by new entrepreneurs setting up their own business and recruiting those people who are losing their own jobs via the cuts. There is still a very high profile push to bring people off of incapacity benefits and of course there is a link here: let us help people to set up in business who have been on benefits- either unemployment or incapacity. Whilst advice, support and expertise is available from a multitude of sources, the biggest single thing that individuals really need is continuation of funding- and a small start-up fund PRIOR to launch.

Such a programme does not exist and some previously helpful discretionary funds and programmes have actually been cut. I talked about this issue in more detail on my blog at the LGA but whilst we are all aware of the need for cost reduction and budget redress, we are also aware of the importance of small businesses in our economy. Therefore, hitting the job-creation sector is not only a grave error, it is the very opposite of what is needed. Britain needs new small businesses to launch, it needs existing small businesses to grow, and it needs strong community and 3rd sector groups (as envisaged in The Big Society, remember that?) to be able to take on community services that can no longer be afforded by statutory agencies.

Even a hugely successful programme run by A4e providing support, training and 12 weeks financial support to those wanting to return to work by setting up their own business was cut by the Government, who, it is alleged, said the reason it had to be cut was because it had been *too* successful (i.e. it was running over budget).

Now, I don't know about you, but finding an extra £1m or so to help people come off of benefits, set up a business, bring money into the local economy and hopefully hire local people as their business grows sounds like a good investment to me, especially if we all agree that it will be small businesses that provide the growth we need to pull out of the financial issues faced as a nation when we rely on the City of London to generate wealth for the rest of the country (what a con that is!).

But here's the problem: our Government (and by this, I mean *ANY* government) operates in a discontinuity mode. The Department for Justice has to make cuts as does the Department for Work & Pensions. So they set about making cuts that, because they're not co-ordinated into a bigger picture, completely affect the programmes run by the Department for Trade & Industry. In effect, cuts in one department can cause significant rises in the expenditures of others.

The question therefore becomes: do you recognise this within your own organisation?

Does a policy affected by your accounts department increase their efficiency whilst slowing down your sales people? Is a new picking system implemented by your operations and warehousing team causing problems with the accountancy system? Is a great and fantastic marketing campaign causing problems because you don't have enough sales support staff in place to sift through and validate the responses before your sales people can get to the call before it goes cold? Does the IT department consult with the office maintenance department about how the new Okicokie3000 Tower PC will integrate with the office furniture, power supply set up and so on?

It is imperative that everyone in your organisation thinks of their wider connection to the rest of the organisation before rolling out their amazing new system, or changes the rules, or implements a new process or even reveals a new product or service.

That means implementing a change management board made up of representatives from all areas of your business, to evaluate any proposed changes to any system that operates within the business. Want to launch a new service? Have it checked out by your operations, financial and IT staff to make sure their systems are fully up to speed. Want to put in a speedier accountancy package, check it's not going to create extra paperwork for the sales staff that needs to be selling, not filling in forms. And so on.

Words of Wisdom

"Quantum physics thus reveals a basic oneness of the universe." Erwin Schrödinger

This also means of course that you have to bring all your departmental heads on board and convince them of the need for such considerations and evaluations to be made. And then you have the ego battles to deal with. However, if you've already worked with the team on creating your vision and subsequent business plan, you can keep bringing them back to that to refocus their mental capacity onto what can they do to achieve the vision and company objectives, rather than on who's got the biggest, er, department. In other words, when the bickering starts you ask them *what is the vision for the company?* When they answer, you add, "So how is this dispute moving us along to making that vision a reality? It doesn't, so let's get back to it shall we?"

Keep that kind of chastisement up and eventually even the biggest ego-heads will start to focus on what they need to focus on and not on their own agenda.

You could even go so far as to just do a wacky tree-hugging session with your entire organisation, starting with the James Lovelock video presentation on YouTube and then explaining why you are showing them the video and how you want the culture of the business to change. Get your employees to then engage in exercises that make them think about how their role interconnects with every other role within the company. And encourage everyone to start with the idea of people at the centre of it all.

Like all major changes, don't just make this a one off event; make sure it is followed up with mini-talks, email reminders, competitions, and so on. Once it is established within your organisation you then need to extend the Gaia Principle to incorporate your suppliers and your customers.

Take a bite...

Call a meeting with your department heads and ask them to each take it in turns to reveal any changes they are thinking of making, or are making, in their processes, systems or staffing rotas etc., and then go round the table and ask each member to assess if the change will have an impact on their department. If you're a team manager or one-person band, start to think about changes you may want to make, or have been told you need to make, and analyse thoroughly. Make sure you communicate any concerns.

Think about this. If you have a client who is just a client (or perceives that's what they are), how loyal to your organisation do you think they will be? Let me rephrase that: how easy would it be for that client to move their business elsewhere? For example, if a new purchasing manager may be brought in who has always dealt with XYZ Ltd before, how easy could that manager simply re-route the orders?

However, if your client was considered by everyone within your organisation to be part of your own eco-system, and this started to translate not only into how the client was physically treated by your staff at every level of contact so that they knew they were part of your eco-system, but also into incorporation into your infrastructure (for example, an extranet where information and orders were passed quickly and easily between you), how easy would it be for that client to simply move to a competitor then? In fact, would they even consider it? Furthermore, if on visits to your offices, they could see an environment where staff had space to think, were encouraged to talk and share ideas and experiences, and could see how all this created a buzz in the office that drove how they interacted with staff at their offices, wouldn't that be amazing? Wouldn't they want to know how your company does it? Is there an opportunity to make your client feel even more beholden to your company?

This is the power of truly embracing The Gaia Principle.

Try something else...

This Principle is of course extremely powerful when combined with Principle 5: The Round Table Principle.

Principle 11: The Gaia Principle in Summary.

Everything in your organisation is connected to everything else in your organisation, and changes to one element can have ramifications to others.

Coping with indigestion?

Q: I still think this is a bit hippy-hug-a-tree. Are you sure this idea would work in a business context?

A: Yes.

> I was just going to leave this answer as that, a simple yes, but my editor wouldn't let me, so let me expand a little more. It would work simply because creating a culture where your

employees (and eventually suppliers and clients) started to view their organisation as a living, breathing entity, would mean that most of them would have a subconscious drive to take care of that entity. It all comes back to the idea that the more a person feels a positive connection to an organisation, the more loyal they will be to it, and the more determined they will be to make it a success.

Furthermore, even simple changes can bring about improved finances. For example Bank of America, trying to discover why some of its call centres were performing so much better than others, fitted workers with a tracking device so it could monitor their habits. To their surprise they found that the centres where workers were more sociable within the office were far more productive. So they set up a company-wide scheme to promote a culture of taking more breaks, and the centres became 10% more productive. Remember however, simply telling people to take breaks isn't enough, you have to design into your office space facilities that enable staff to take breaks in a relaxing and sociable way.

And what about creating a thinking space for your employees too? If they could make a cuppa and have 15 minutes in an area designed to encourage reflection and thinking, wouldn't there be the occasional gem of brilliance that could be of huge benefit to your department or company?

Just by creating a thinking process that links aspects of your business together, rather than taking a departmental one at a time approach, can reap huge benefits!

Principle 12

The 99 Monkeys Principle!
Create change by setting the trend!

You've asked the unthinkable question and identified potential threats. And you have decided that maybe prevention is better than the cure, and you want it to be your organisation that changes the rules of the game. So how do you go about it?

A famous experiment conducted in 1952 on an island with monkeys that had not experienced human contact found that a strange shared consciousness appeared to exist between the monkeys once a critical mass was reached.[71]

The behaviour of the Japanese monkey Macaca (or Macaco depending on whether you use the French or Portuguese term) fuscata was studied intensely for more than thirty years in a number of wild colonies, one of which was based on the island of Koshimajust off the east coast of Kyushu.

---

[71] Full details are in the book 'Lifetide', by Lyall Watson. Book Club Associates, London, 1979. The description of the experiment paraphrases pages 155-158.

The naturalists quickly established that young monkeys learned their feeding habits from their mothers who teach them by example what to eat and how to deal with it. This system had evolved to incorporate a sophisticated set of routines and habits when dealing with the indigenous plants and vegetables. The team therefore decided to introduce a number of artificial food supplies, including raw sweet potatoes covered with sand and grit. At first the monkeys were unable to adapt their routines to cope with the potato until an eighteen month old female, called Imo, solved the problem by carrying the potatoes down to a stream and washing them before feeding. As Lyall Watson observes: "In monkey terms this is a cultural revolution comparable almost to the invention of the wheel. It involves abstraction, the identification of concept, and deliberate manipulation of several parameters in the environment."

Words of Wisdom

"A crank is someone with a new idea, until it catches on." Mark Twain

Imo then taught the trick to her mother. She also taught it to her playmates and they in their turn spread the news to their mothers. Slowly, step by step, a new culture spread through the colony, with each new conversion taking place in full view of the observers who kept a constant watch right through all the daylight hours. By 1958, all the juvenile monkeys were washing any dirty food, not just the salt and grit covered potatoes, although the number of adults to do so were the ones who learned by direct imitation from their children.

In the autumn of that year an unspecified number of monkeys on Koshima were washing sweet potatoes in the sea, because Imo had made the further discovery that salt water not only cleaned the food but gave it an interesting new flavour. Gradually this number increased until one day, roughly 100 monkeys were actively involved in this cleaning process.

This last addition however caused something spectacular to occur. As the number of monkeys increased, they were carried across some sort of threshold, pushing it through a kind of critical mass because by the evening of that same day of 100th conversion, almost everyone in the colony was doing it. Not only that, but the habit then appeared to jump natural barriers and to occur spontaneously in colonies on other islands and on the mainland in a troop at Takasakiyama.

Why is this? What occurred that so after years of slow build up that sudden massive change literally happened over night?

No-one is entirely sure, even now, but many scientists, philosophers and ecologists point to the idea of some kind of shared consciousness that exists. Such thinking of course might well explain how fads and trends occur: as soon as a critical mass of people experience the fad, it jumps nationally and in a lot of cases internationally.

So how does all this relate to business?

Consider this, what if you could be that 100th Monkey, the one that notices what the other 99 monkeys are doing and acts as the catalyst to create a new movement for change, or a new market place for certain products or services? How much of a competitive edge would that be to you?

Take a bite...

With this Principle there is no easy step up, you simply have to bite the bullet and jump in (I know, mixing my metaphors, but you know what I mean!). Get together with likeminded people or company staff and analyse your market place by using the 5 stages following on page 237. Act upon the results!

There are of course many ways to do trend analysis and there are many resources out there that can help, such as books like 'Trend Tracking' by Gerald Celente and Tom Milton, and trend forecasters such as Faith Popcorn and The Brain Reserve (yes I know it sounds like a pop band), so I am not going to go into any great detail here[72].

However, a simple way to spot a trend before it occurs is to monitor when a sea change begins to happen in the way people begin to challenge the status quo. In other words, what questions are a significant number of people asking about any aspect of life, government, commerce etc, that no more than a couple of years ago would have been unthinkable?

Linked to this, and a great area to focus on, is what alternatives are these people starting to look at? In other words, if people appear to be deciding that banks are so evil they want to keep their money under their mattress, are you able to develop a secure home banking system that can capitalise on this growing trend and be first to market with a solution? I am only half talking with tongue in cheek of course. If enough people decide to boycott businesses that are connected to any kind of obscene bonus scheme, how can you market yourself in such a way that those people will come and deal with you as their alternative?

Ask also, what rules are being broken? What service or product could you deliver that could enable these rule breakers to do so in comfort or style?

Why is it important to spot trends? Simple, if you get in quick enough (and for fads, get out even faster) you can generate enormous revenues for your business.

If you can create a trend that is even better. The way to create a trend is to perform the five step process as illustrated on the next page, and then build upon a slowly increasing number of potential clients who

---

[72] There is also a powerful audio book from Tony Robbins on creating change- see Power Talk Vol 20.

appear to be moving in that direction by getting your product or service ready, and adding/directing your own clients and suppliers toward the trend you wish to initiate. Starting a trend is much more difficult than spotting a trend before it takes off. However there are five stages a new trend will go through before it becomes "active", and if you understand these stages then it makes the actual creation easier to perform.

These stages are as follows:

Stage 1: Enough people have to get into enough pain to want to make a change. We have seen this I the last decade with the furore in the UK over the MPs expenses scandal and bankers bonuses. Despite incredible (and unbelievable) resistance from the establishment, changes were forced through[73]. What pain could you create in the minds of people who could be interested in your products or services?

Stage 2: Enough people start to question the unquestionable. That is, a critical mass of people ask questions that force a reaction from the establishment. What question could you start to ask, and how could you get enough people to notice the question so they ask it too?

Stage 3: Enough people start to search for a new alternative. Bottled water is a great example of this. People became so worried about the quality of tap water that a whole industry was literally created over night. What is happening at the moment that you can capitalise on with a new product or service?

Stage 4: People start to adopt a new set of rules (or break existing ones). The sit-in movement, which grew almost exponentially as I wrote the original version of this book, is a prime example of this. People were passively breaking rules and laws because they had enough of the rampant rabid form of capitalism that has destroyed so many lives. What can you do to create a rule change?

---

[73] Sadly, the establishment has focused our rage onto other groups and quietly rolled back these changes…

Stage 5: When enough people adopt the new rules, new behaviours appear and a new trend is created. This one is self-explanatory and only occurs after the first four stages have completed.

Keep monitoring the growing activity that supports the trend you want to create, and then be the 100th Monkey. Create that critical mass that suddenly launches the trend into the public consciousness, and launch your product or service at that precise moment. After all, as Peter Drucker said; "The best way to predict the future is to create it."

Try something else...

If the thought of being in command of your environment makes you feel all tingly you should check out Principle 6: The Unexpected Guest Principle.

Principle 12: The 99 Monkeys Principle in Summary.

Trends and fads could come into being simply by a new shared consciousness created by a critical mass of people spreading the idea. What you must do is learn how to anticipate such new trends and capitalise on them as they occur.

Coping with indigestion?

Q: If it's easy to anticipate trends, why isn't everyone doing it?

A: *Well, I didn't exactly say it's easy to anticipate trends, let alone create them. What I did say is that if you understand how trends are created, then it becomes less difficult to spot them in embryonic state. It's still a lot of bloody hard work and not all your predictions will come true. But the rewards are huge when you do get it right.*

Conclusion

Think of this as the coffee and nightcap.

Next Steps

In this book are 18 areas to focus on and 12 Principles to consider, weigh up and apply. Each of these 30 ideas and strategies also incorporate literally dozens of tools, actions and practical steps to take. So how do you begin?

"The only way to discover the limits of what is possible is to go beyond them into the impossible." AC Clarke

My recommendation is to do the following:

1. Don't try to do everything at once. Pick those areas that seem initially most applicable and master them first.
2. Assess the weakest area of your business right now and apply the tools and strategies that are directly relevant. For example, if you have never considered what might be a threat to your company outside of your normal competition, work through The Unexpected Guest Principle and apply the actions contained therein. And then follow the thread through the "Try Something Else" sections.
3. Assess the *strongest* area of your business and apply the relevant tools and strategies to enhance what you are currently achieving. For example if you already have a fantastic employee suggestions and encouragement system in place, build upon it by applying The Round Table Principle and follow the subsequent thread to be found in the "Try Something Else" section.
4. Understand that whilst this book is designed to be easy to follow and provide you with huge benefits, nothing beats having a live, interactive session to really flesh out the ideas and concepts. At the most basic level, if you run some of the suggested workshops, you must make sure you have a fantastic workshop invigilator who understands what is required. That does not have to be me- there are some amazing people out there who can do an outstanding job, and maybe even someone in your organisation is one of those people. Just don't do this on the cheap.
5. Do utilise the money saving vouchers in this book. I can guarantee action packed, fun and incredibly valuable sessions.

That's it. Good luck and let me know what successes you've had using these Principles. You could be featured in future versions of the book!

Final Words

I hope you've enjoyed reading this book and that you'll apply, with an open mind, the actions, tools and thinking I've incorporated into it.

Remember, this book is a distillation of over 25 years of experience and thinking and whilst much of it may appear a direct contradiction to what you know and have been told over the years about how business should be run, I stand by EVERY word and idea you'll find in it.

Now, if you're asking do I perfectly apply each and every one of these Principles I have to admit no I don't. I am only human, and many of these Principles have arisen out of some disastrous mistakes I have made throughout my career! What I am trying to do is stop others from making the same, painful errors whilst also trying to create a critical mass of likeminded people who want to change the rules of the game[74]. In short, I am definitely getting better at applying on a daily basis these Principles, and it's in those times that I don't that I get bitten in the ass.

"You see things and say 'why?'; but I dream of things that never were and I say, 'why not?'. George Bernard Shaw

And I hope you'll forgive me a moment of selling: If you have enjoyed the book, and see the value in what I am trying to do, make sure to book me to come do your client event as a Keynote Speaker. Imagine getting your clients switched onto some of these strategies and giving you all the credit for introducing you to them! Or book me to workshop your organisation.

That's it. All that remains for me to do is to say:

Here's to Magic. Long may it burn within us and turn us all into rebels in the FDG.

Darren Smithson

August 2015

---

[74] Quick, which Principle does this relate to!!!?

Special Offers (or, The Dessert!)

As a reward for buying this book and putting up with my rants, the next few pages contain some vouchers that you can use with The Inform Group.

All you have to do is quote the number on the voucher and who you are (so we can check you really did buy this book and didn't just illegally copy it from your colleague!).

Voucher 1.

25% off What Managers Don't Know Workshops.

This provides fully one quarter off interactive or keynote sessions on the ideas, Principles and suggested activities discussed within this book, including:

- The Unexpected Guest Principle
- The Round Table Principle
- The 99 Monkeys Principle
- And so on, including the Focus Areas.

NOTE: The workshop sessions usually take a half day for each Principle, whilst the keynote talks take 45 minutes to give a quick overview of the 12 principles.

Quote Number: V1TCWMDK

Voucher 2.

25% off Business Keynote Speaking & Training Courses

This provides fully one quarter off the current keynote speeches and/or lectures we do, including:

- 5 Top Things That Can Kill Your Business- and how to avoid them!
- Holding out for a Hero: Self Motivation without the Psychobabble
- "The 7 Deadly Sins of Presenting and How To Exorcise Them"
- "The Top 5 Reasons Projects Fail"
- "5 Ways to Lose Your Customers"
- Resurrecting The Digital Nervous System: Why a 1990s Market Spoiler Could Lead To Success Today

Note: You can book me to do these sessions directly for your own organisation, or to offer me as value added service to your clients.

Quote Number: V2KNS

Voucher 3.

25% off Fun Keynote Speaking.

This provides fully one quarter off the current keynote speeches and/or lectures we do in an educational context but which you can use at your internal conferences or client functions to be a little different, including:

- "I'm Sorry Dave, I'm Afraid I Can't Do That"- Robots and Artificial Intelligence in Fact & Fiction"
- "There's an Elephant on my head and other tales from the multiverse"- The Many Worlds Theory
- "Time is Nature's Way of Stopping Everything From Happening At Once: Discuss"- theories of time and time travelling
- "This Island Earth: The Search for Alien Life"
- "Multiple Earth Mashup: Superheroes and the story of the multiverse" (a version of There's An Elephant, but using Superman and Supergirl stories etc to explain the science)
- Of Neutrinos, Tachyons and Relativity: was Einstein Wrong?

Note: You do not have to have any scientific experience to enjoy and understand these sessions.

Quote Number: V3KNF

Voucher 4.

33% off Project Management Services.

This provides fully one third off the current Project Management Services that we offer.

Quote Number: V4PMS

www.ingramcontent.com/pod-product-compliance
Lightning Source LLC
Chambersburg PA
CBHW051638170526
45167CB00001B/243